I0683389

EXPERIENCING PSYCHOTHERAPY THROUGH A ONE-WAY WINDOW

....115 VIGNETTES FROM REAL LIFE SESSIONS OF PSYCHOTHERAPY WITH A THERAPIST....

ALLAN G. HEDBERG, Ph.D.

CLINICAL PSYCHOLOGIST

YOU ARE INVITED......... TO PERSONALLY OBSERVE AND BENEFIT FROM 115 PSYCHOTHERAPY SESSIONS THROUGH A ONE-WAY WINDOW WITH THERAPIST DR. HEDBERG, CLINICAL PSYCHOLOGIST

ATTEND. LEARN. BENEFIT.

It is always a good thing to learn from others and even learn from the mistakes of others. Indeed, I learn every day from every patient. It is a cycle of experience.... learning from each other and passing it on. Truly, that is *"giving psychology away"*.... The guiding theme of my professional career.

Copyright © 2024 by ALLAN G. HEDBERG, Ph.D.

ISBN: 979-8-89465-068-5 (sc)
ISBN: 979-8-89465-069-2 (e)

All rights reserved. No part of this publication may be reproduced, distributed, or transmitted in any form or by any means, including photocopying, recording, or other electronic or mechanical methods, without the prior written permission of the author, except in the case of brief quotations embodied in critical reviews and certain other noncommercial uses permitted by copyright law.

Printed in the United States of America.

Integrity Publishing
39343 Harbor Hills Blvd Lady Lake,
FL 32159

www.integrity-publishing.com

ACKNOWLEDGEMENTS

No book comes together by itself or as a result of one man's efforts. Every book is the result to many individuals working towards the common goal for a book's publication. This book is no different. The same applies to one's professional career. Many individuals played a role over the years of my studies, internships, practicums, teaching assistantships, and my first job assignment as an elementary school teacher in Western Springs, Illinois.

A special and appreciation are due to my father, the first person to suggest to me that I might do well in psychology and should consider a major in psychology for my studies in college. At the time, I was floundering and debating if law should be my area of study. After my talk with dad, I went into psychology and never turned back. That was during my first year in college, Wright Community College in Chicago.

Once I started down that path of studies, I was subsequently affirmed by many professors along the way..... Drs. Edith Grotberg, Bond Woodruff, Erwin Lotsof, John Knowles, James Sutherland, Wilda Andreski, Arthur Arthur, Ernest Poser, Jerry Wilde, and Joseph Wolpe, to name a few.

I am also grateful to several student colleagues who challenged me each day in the classroom and from assignment to assignment .... David Homes, Dennis Olenik, Ed Bauman, Joe McSpadden, David Senn, and David Miller, to name a few.

I also reflect on several students who achieved the doctorate degree under my teaching and professional mentorship ... Lowell Campbell, Mike Fitts, Michael Kesselman, Brent Lindquist, Ronald Meredith, Steven Younker, and Barbara Knowles, among others. Each went on to distinguish themselves in their field of service as a doctoral level psychologist.

Further, I have had the privilege of serving our community along with several other professional psychologists, such as, Drs. Stanley Lindquist, Steve Younker, Deborah Ohanesian, Michael Kesselman, Sharon Johnson, Bradley Schuyler, and Mary Watts, LCSW.

On the administrative side, I am always thankful for my secretarial team of Kathy Hamlin, Gina Berry, and my wife, Bernice. Kathy did all the typing of the original manuscript. Kathy and my wife did the first draft's proof-reading. Gina helped with the computer hang-ups. I took over from there and put the finishing touches together. Forgive any remaining typos and dangling participles.

Appreciation is also extended to Rob Carey for his art work and design assistance. Rob is acknowledged for his international acclaim as a sketcher.

Recently, our community was caused to reflect on the teaching and writings of Janice Stevens. She was a delightful mid-age woman who succumbed to the deadly effects of cancer as her career was still growing. Janice taught hundreds of students the skill of writing while capturing the joy of writing, as well. She and her colleague, Pat Hunter, became a legacy in Central California for their writings and art. Together, they were an example of a team capturing the essence of nature and history through word, watercolor, and oil We will miss Janice and her ongoing influence in putting history into meaningful word pictures. I will miss her inspiration and writing guidance.

A special thanks to the many patients whose stories I captured and summarized here in this volume for the benefit of every reader who did not participate in therapy with me directly. Also, thanks to the thousands of patients I have seen and guided in their life over the past fifty years, even if I did not use their story.

Everyone's story is a personal story and can't be replicated. However, we can learn from each other as we share experiences and personal events that otherwise would not come to the surface for the benefit of others.

The stories in this book are meant for your learning and edification. All stories are real and personal. As you read, please learn and apply the lessons to your life as they are relevant. You need not be concerned with the person whose story it is, but focus on the lesson to be learned within the story.

Hopefully, you will be encouraged to tell your own story to someone who can benefit from it. Encourage others to read the book. Hopefully, the book will encourage them to tell their story so someone else who can profit from it as well. Learn a variety of ways to tell your own story. Gain the courage to help others write their story and be prepared to help them tell their own story also.

With Respect,
Allan G. Hedberg, Ph.D.

CONTENTS

PART II: CAN THERAPY HELP ME DEAL WITH MY PROBLEMS?   29

PART III: CAN THERAPY HELP ME OVERCOME DISCOURAGEMENT?   51

PART VII: CAN THERAPY HELP ME BETTER RESPOND TO SIGNIFICANT LIFE-CHANGING EVENTS?   129

PART XI: CAN THERAPY HELP ME KNOW HOW TO HELP MY KIDS DO WELL IN SCHOOL?   197

PART XII: CAN THERAPY HELP ME OVERCOME MY ADDICTION?   207

INTRODUCTION

Going to a therapist or engaging in psychotherapy, family therapy, or some form of counseling has historically been off limits. In fact, it has generally been an area of life that is associated with fear and other unwanted feelings. Going to a therapist has generally been something that was very private and kept as one of the secrets of life.

Further, in the past, therapists have been viewed as being quirks, quacks, odd individuals, and, therefore, should be avoided. To be sure, most therapists do not fit that mold. Some do. In fact, therapists have been found to be no different than anyone else that you include in your circle of friendships or those you consult professionally. They are no different than the personality and style of life of your physician, dentist, accountant, attorney, minister, or mortician.

However, over recent years therapy has become more commonplace and acceptable than has ever been the case in history. Going to a therapist has become no different than consulting a physician, or an accountant whom you consult regarding your taxes and other financial matters, or even a dentist to whom you entrust your teeth on a regular basis.

Accordingly, this book resulted out of the relaxed attitude that has emerged over recent years, whereas going to a therapist has become commonplace and acceptable. In fact, patients are known to share information with others from their therapy sessions.

Research has been conducted on the happiness level of different professionals. The psychologist comes out on top. Accordingly, a psychologist need not be avoided as he/she generally is happier and the experience spent with a therapist is generally found to be a happy experience.

So, I welcome you into my office by reading the various vignettes offered in this book. Each vignette is real and represents real life experiences in therapy. You can learn from others. You can learn from the mistakes of others. You can learn from the advice and the corresponding changes that take place as a result of therapy. You are invited to eavesdrop into the therapy office through these vignettes, in which all names and identification factors of the patients have been changed.

It is my hope that you will not only read and benefit from the various vignettes contained in this book, but will be encouraged to engage in and participate in your own therapy program with a therapist of your choice. Find one with whom you feel compatible and have commonality. Find one that is trained and experienced in the issues you are dealing with and would like to explore and assist you in making changes in your life.

Also, note that each vignette ends with a piece of advice. Now, I am aware that unsolicited advice is usually unwelcomed advice and therefore rejected. I would ask that you read each statement with an open mind. See what you can learn from the "unsolicited advice" after each vignette.

Lastly, it is interesting to note that research indicates that most patients, male and female, prefer female therapists. If that is your case, make sure you seek out a female therapist with whom you can consult and whom you trust. Don't overlook the male therapists in your area. There are many good ones. On the other hand, that does not necessarily indicate that female therapists are better or would be more helpful to you. A preference for a particular therapist does not indicate that the therapist will provide the service, the assistance, and help that you need and are seeking. However, it's a good place to start.

It is important to recall some recent and relevant research on the topic of choosing a doctor when needed. Three points stand out for best results to be obtained: 1) You must like your doctor, 2) You must trust your doctor, and 3) You must feel compatible with your doctor. If these factors are not present, go find another doctor. If they are present, be thankful and submit yourself to an enriching personal growth experience. Finally, start by reading selected vignettes on the personal growth experiences of other patients, similarly situated to yourself. I wish you well in your venture of self-improvement.............

Allan G. Hedberg, Ph.D.

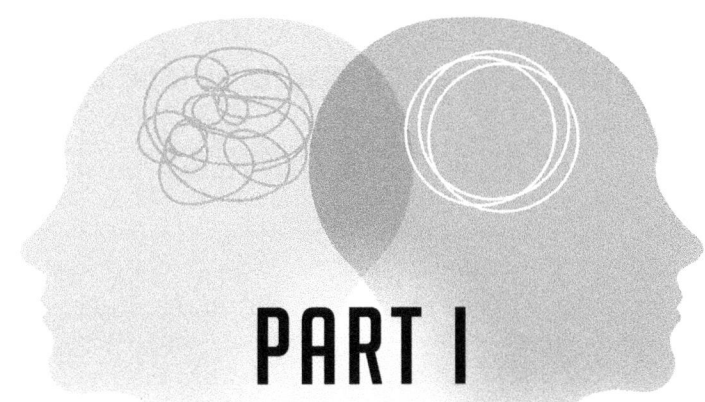

PART I

UNDERSTANDING THE THERAPIST AND THE PSYCHOTHERAPY PROCESS

1.
THERAPISTS KEEP THEIR SKILLS AND KNOWLEDGE CURRENT

As a professional psychologist, it is incumbent upon me to actively engage in an ongoing educational process within the field of psychology, as well as in other relevant areas outside the boundaries of psychology such as philosophy, anthropology, sociology, theology, and other areas often considered quite different from psychology as a field of study. Every patient deserves to have services provided that are up-to-date and consistent with current research and are medically and psychologically verifiable. A therapist should "follow the science" by studying current developments in the field of psychology and beyond.

Patients have the right to ask their therapist about their educational experience and background and what they are doing to maintain their educational knowledge base. For example, beyond formal training, psychologists are required to participate in 36 hours every two years of continuing professional development. Beyond that, a psychologist on their own should maintain an active reading program, attend lectures, participate in workshops and educational programs, communicate with those who are experts in the field of psychology, and even go back to school and upgrade their education in some new area of interest and specialization.

First and foremost, a psychologist is a student of knowledge, science, and all fields relevant to the unique problems patients bring to the therapy sessions. Patients should demand no less. Patients should know that when they seek the counsel of a psychologist as their therapist they are seeking the counsel of a wise person, a learned person, a caring person, and a therapist who is current in his understanding of relevant research and methods to promote healing and behavior change. Patients should expect a therapist to be well-versed and experienced in the very concerns the patient brings to therapy at a time of need.

If a therapist is not trained, experienced, or educated in the needed therapeutic methods and approaches, a referral to another therapist who is trained and experienced would be appropriate and ethical.

MY COMMENT: Seek the counsel of a therapist who is well-educated, experienced, and demonstrates advanced knowledge and experience.

2.
THERAPISTS MUST TAKE CARE OF THEMSELVES TO HELP OTHERS

It is important for a therapist to engage in a systematic program of self-care. To do so honors the patient he or she serves as well as his or her profession. Burnout is potentially on the horizon for every therapist. Preventative action must be undertaken in a systematic manner so burn out does not develop. Effective service to a patient population day upon day requires stamina, endurance, motivation, interest, focus, and an up-to-date knowledge base. Hence, a therapist must be proactive in following a comprehensive professional development and a self-care action plan.

While every therapist has his or her own system of self-care, there are several fundamental steps that all therapists engage in to prevent burnout and to keep professionally fresh and effective. Consider the following examples:

1. Participate in an active continuing education program. Professional knowledge and career development are a necessary feature of ongoing effectiveness.

2. Take frequent mini-vacations. It is important to take at least four, if not five or six vacations a year which need not be more than three to five days at a time. To be sure, several mini-vacations are better than one long vacation.

3. Have friends and associates that are not in the field of counseling. This gives experimental richness, diversity of thought, and variety to life. Thinking about non-psychology problems and a broad base of information exposure is vital to any creative and productive activity, such as counseling.

4. Read widely. Read on topics of psychology and counseling, but also include topics such as history, biographies, short stories, philosophy, and ethics, to name few.

5. Maintain a healthy life style, including exercise, relaxation, healthy eating, controlled use of alcohol and abstinence from all drugs and other addictive behavior patterns.

6. Never engage in any behavior or activities that have consequences and will change the course of one's life forever.

If it is important to you as a patient that your therapist engages in a program of professional development and self-care; feel free to inquire. It is important that you feel comfortable with your therapist and that you trust your therapist. According to recent research, your outcome will be more assured if you settle this issue from the beginning and start with confidence.

MY COMMENT: A therapist who actively engages in self-care is good for you.

3.
THE LIFE OF A THERAPIST CAN BE AN EXAMPLE

I take my therapy sessions seriously with all my patients. As part of this, it is important that I, as a therapist, maintain a healthy lifestyle and live a balanced life. Accordingly, years ago I committed myself and have followed the pattern of healthy living which includes:

- Daily exercise and attendance at the local gym on a regular basis.

- Maintain a life of faith through church attendance and participation.

- Adequate sleep.

- Augment my physical health through the use of vitamins, Omega-3, and Vitamin D3.

- Avoid exposing myself to high levels of risk or dangerous living.

- Maintain a broad range of social connections and friends.

- Avoid and abstain from any and all habit-forming or addictive behavior patterns.

- Maintain a vacation schedule of at least four breaks a year, at least four days each.

- Take in relaxing community events such as the Philharmonic and various athletic events.

The above list works for me. But, it also is a list to recommend to patients that engage in diverse and stressful living as well, and therefore, need to live healthy and well. Patients not only need a nudge, but sometimes need an example. We learn from examples. We need examples to imitate and to give us direction and encouragement to proceed. I try to be that kind of example with my patients without boasting.

MY COMMENT: Live healthy; follow the example of your therapist.

4.
COMMONALITY WITH YOUR THERAPIST MAY AID PROGRESS

Psychotherapy is built on the premise that the patient and doctor come together on certain commonalities and share some aspect of a mutual story. From that builds trust. Trust is the basis for a person to open their lives and share it with another person. That's what psychotherapy is all about. It's important for me as a therapist to give enough information about myself so that a bond is established, a bridge is built, a mutual interest is identified, and things we enjoy in common are shared. From this trust results.

Patients often learn things about the therapist's personal life and background. Usually, they do not find it offensive, but rather as a way to feel connected as they share mutual experiences. This occurs over time and several sessions.

For example, just this past week I had two occasions of talking with patients in which one patient and I had a common location and activity for a vacation. It was an unusual location and included an unusual activity. I've never found another patient sharing this common interest with me, let alone friends and people I've met elsewhere. The uniqueness seemed to just draw us together and share a deeper moment in our relationship. In fact, it facilitated the therapy.

With the second patient, in our discussion we found that we had a common city in another country where we both spent time. He lived there for a period of time. I visited the city over twenty-five times. It was like coming home together. Again, there are indications of this common experience that brought us together, gained a good laugh, and opened a door for an interesting topic of discussion which had therapeutic value.

It is important in such situations that boundaries be maintained, and a sense of dignity be preserved and honored. Yes, some sharing, but the distinctives of the relationship needs to be maintained.

MY COMMENT: Be open and share your life experience, but be discreet.

5.
WRITTEN HANDOUTS ARE ALWAYS APPRECIATED BY PATIENTS

Over the years of my clinical practice, I have written and made available to patients over 150 papers on specific topics such as depression, anxiety, positive marital relationships, styles of communication, and other such topics. When a topic in therapy comes around to one of these issues, I am then able to provide a handout to the patient to take home and read during the course of the next week or two. Handouts provide a very helpful adjunct to the therapy process and to the gains and changes that are desired in therapy.

Parents like such handouts to use with their kids. They also work great for couples who are learning better ways of relating to each other in their daily personal lives. If you are in therapy, ask your therapist for any relevant handouts or if he has any books he recommends. Be sure to obtain information that is relevant to your situation. Read it and discuss it with someone. Also, come prepared to discuss it at the next therapy session.

Here are some of the topics that have been popular and helpful to patients:

- Depression Comes to the Office
- Overcoming Fear
- Assertive Communication Skills
- Dealing with an Angry Child
- Controlling Anxiety
- Managing Pain
- Becoming More Independent

I have also found these papers to be helpful when I am asked to speak to some particular audience, such as a company staff meeting. Such handouts serve as the general topic and give structure when time is limited.

MY COMMENT: Ask your therapist for any handouts and articles so you can benefit while you wait for your next appointment.

6.
TELL YOUR STORY TO A THERAPIST CONFIDENTIALLY

It is not uncommon to have long held secrets unfolded by a patient during a therapy session. Actually, there are many patients who come to therapy with a secret and are wanting to unfold that secret so they can remove it from their emotional memory and also remove the associated physical and emotional pain.

However, when a patient comes with a secret, it is not until about the fourth or fifth session before it is revealed. A trust level must be established. The patient must feel that you will not only maintain confidentiality, but will help them cope with that secret. They need to learn that you are capable and competent to deal with the particular secret they would like to unfold to you.

Some patients never tell a secret, but only refer to an "experience" or "event" in a vague and generalized manner. Certainly, a patient does not want to be condemned, put down, degraded, or diminished in any way because of the event which prompted the formation of the secret in the first place.

Secrets cause pain. Most secrets are nearly impossible to tell someone even if that person can be of help. Secrets represent a major source of stress and can be responsible for a life of medical and behavioral malfunction. I recall one lady who came to therapy indicating she had a secret with which to deal. She never did tell me the secret, but after three sessions in which it was alluded to, she stated she felt better and felt she had adequately resolved the conflict within oneself about her secret. We talked around the issue, but not about it.

It should be noted that a secret is different from a personal matter that is not to be shared. A personal matter does not imply that a wrong has been committed but rather it is a matter of personal embarrassment.

Obviously, over my years fifty years of practice I have heard many secrets. I can understand why a secret is a secret and must be protected. Patients holding a secret want to be protected. This is equally true whether you see a patient in family therapy, marital therapy, or individual therapy.

Secrets tend to be related to character issues, integrity issues, and fidelity issues. Occasionally, they tend to be of a legal nature raising the question as to the legal obligation of a therapist to report a criminal action. Outside of child abuse, reporting an action for criminal consideration is rare. A real and specific threat to do harm to someone targeted is an exception and needs to be reported in a very specific way for the protection of the parties involved.

Every therapist must be knowledgeable and well-versed as to when a particular historical event, often a secret, requires a criminal report outside of child abuse. Otherwise, it is resolved or clarified within the structures of therapy!

It needs to be pointed out that therapists have an obligation, by law, to maintain confidentiality. This is ironclad. Patients must be informed and reassured of it when they start in therapy.

MY COMMENT: Secrets are self-defeating and can cause much pain; resolve them while you have professional guidance.

7.
USING JOURNALING ALONG WITH THERAPY BRINGS MAXIMUM BENEFIT

Psychological research has well demonstrated a positive role for journaling in the course of therapy with a patient. Patients tend to improve much more quickly and in a positive way if they journal while in therapy.

Accordingly, I wrote a book on journaling for patients entitled *"Park Your Story Here."* It provides a series of questions and areas of life for a person to give consideration to and write his or her personal story on whatever theme seems to be most helpful and appropriate at the time.

I encourage patients to journal. I often review entries that a patient has written regarding their own life to bring about a positive discussion relative to their goals and purpose for being in therapy.

I often provide a copy of my book on journaling to a patient with a series of assignments on topics that I think are relevant and important for the patient's personal growth and development.

Many patients do not feel comfortable or do not have the history of writing. This was the case of Delilah. We had to do it in small incremental baby steps. I gave her a very brief and small assignment, and she carried it out. We then did another. We gradually over time increased the size and the complexity of the assignment.

Delilah gradually experienced the ability to not only write, but to examine her own life and history and more fully participate in her program of recovery.

Writing can help a patient get "unstuck" and enjoy life once again. It helps the patient stay in the moment and yet reflect on history. Writing helps them reflect on their values, balance emotions, gain mental flexibility, and create a pathway of personal growth. Most of all, journaling facilitates the processing of strong emotional experiences such as grief, anger, resentment, betrayal, and false accusations.

MY COMMENT: As your therapist journals, you do likewise and encourage your friends to also journal along with you.

8.
THE FORMAT OF THERAPY MUST BE COMFORTABLE

Individuals who are considering a therapy program for themselves often wonder what it is like and what they can expect to happen. I am not a cookie cutter therapist. Every session is different and every patient is treated differently, depending on their particular situation and issues to be addressed. I recognize that all therapists have their own preferences and format. Patients are urged to discuss with their therapist how therapy might best unfold.

It is not uncommon for therapists to divide their time according to a pre-set schedule or routine. The first few minutes are devoted to informal chit-chat over the events that have transpired in the previous few days to a week. The next thirty-five to forty-five minutes are devoted to the primary purpose of a therapeutic visit. This is followed by five to six minutes in a wrap-up which usually includes the bringing together of the issues discussed thus far in therapy and any related applications and homework that might be indicated.

Many times, during a therapy session, a particular topic or issue comes up that is worthy of extra time and consideration. That was the experience of Andy. He identified an issue that needed to be the focus of attention for the remainder of the third session. That issue took up the majority of the time over the next two or three of his sessions.

So, that is what therapy is all about. Identify the critical issue, dwell on it, and examine it until it is fully resolved. It is important to recognize that each patient has his own manner and sequence of processing issues and problems. The therapist must follow the lead of the patient.

MY COMMENT: Therapy sessions move along quickly. There is never enough time; make good use of it.

9.
THERAPY NEEDS TO END WELL FOR THE PATIENT AND THE THERAPIST

At the end of the session today, Vanessa volunteered two points that we discussed and were helpful to her going forward. That is exactly what each session attempts to accomplish. As a patient gets ready to leave, I try to reflect on the question, "Is there a clear piece of advice or a clearer understanding of an issue that was perplexing or important when therapy started?"

Most patients don't expect life-changing events to happen during the course of one session, but they do expect to have some insight, suggestions, piece of advice, or something to mark progress within a session or between sessions. It could be in the form of a homework assignment, a topic to discuss with the family, spouse, or a friend, a recall of an old but important memory, or an issue put into perspective after speaking with a friend or family member about the issue.

As I write my notes at the end of each session, I try to capture the key issues or key advancements that were made during that particular session. It keeps me in focus and it keeps the therapy session on a theme and having fresh focus as we go forward with future sessions.

Yes, it is best if a therapy session ends on a positive note. Patients need to leave with some good points on which to reflect and come back to discuss further.

MY COMMENT: Always end a conversation or interchange with someone on a point to be remembered or something on which to act.

10.
TALKING ABOUT YOUR STRESSFUL EVENTS IS HELPFUL IN THERAPY

Every time a new patient comes to the office to initiate therapy, I activate my sensitivities relative to their historical story that may well play a critical role in why they are coming now to therapy and how I can be of help to them. Sarah was no exception. She had a very deep and intense story to tell, but you wouldn't know it just looking at her or by just talking with her casually for the first five minutes or so. It wasn't until she felt relaxed, comfortable, and trusting that she was able to give me indications that she had a particular need to tell her story.

First, not only with the people with an obvious story to tell, but with all people, it's important to them that I approach them and begin the session with an attitude of sensitivity, caring, and compassion.

Secondly, it is also important that I slow the process down so that they have time to unfold their story as they lived it. I need to listen intently with the purpose of gaining full understanding of the patients concerns from the start of therapy.

Thirdly, I have to be careful not to jump to conclusions or to immediately move into a posture of directions, suggestions, and ways they should alter their life or deal with the problem. That comes later. But before any action plan is unfolded, comes listening and understanding.

Sarah was no exception. By the end of the third session, she was able to thank me for listening and for caring about her story and what had happened to her. She left with the assurance that at our next session I would want to listen to more detail and for her to unfold more information about certain parts of her story. We could then together look for ways she could move beyond her story and create a new and healthy one. I wanted her to be known not for her past story, but for her new story.

Indeed, therapy is a place to start a new story and to get behavioral change strategies, However, that may come later and after a full understanding of the relevant issues for a patient.

MY COMMENT: Therapy is a place to turn a bad and unhealthy story of your life into a good and healthy story that can be shared for the benefit of others.

11.
THERAPISTS CAN HANDLE INTERPERSONAL CONTROVERSY

It is inevitable that controversial issues are raised during a therapy session. Patients often look to a therapist for wisdom and prudence in handling sticky and controversial issues in society, as well as within family relationships and the many types of informal and friendly relationships into which they enter.

Perhaps the most controversial issue at this time in life is the matter of choice when it comes to certain behavioral patterns. Is it merely choice or is a result of having been born "that way?"

A therapist would be wise not to enter into the controversy by offering just another opinion. Therapists function on the basis of theories of behavior patterns and empirical research on issues and topics. Therapists are wise when they stick to the explanation based on a theory and explanations, based on the research studies that have been conducted thus far on any particular issue. Therapists can offer wisdom and bring reason and calmness to a controversial issue within a person's life, a family, or certainly within our society at large.

When it comes to empirical research, therapists can draw upon surveys that have been conducted, but these are generally a compilation of opinions of people that manifest a trend in thinking as well as in lifestyle of preferences of society. On the other hand, a therapist can defer to well-structured and well-accepted research findings to answer certain questions. In so doing, a therapist draws upon research based on accepted and standard forms of empirical studies. And, a therapist can help patients understand issues through the use of research strategies, such as the mono-zygotic twin studies, when addressing issues such as whether or not gay people are born to be sexually gay. Further, a knowledge of the historical sequence of how certain beliefs came about on a certain controversial issue can also be very helpful in discussing it with a patient who has a strong belief on some point of view, such as the gay life style.

It is essential that a therapist discuss such topics with openness and fairness, and not with sarcasm or controversial intensity.

In other words, psychology is a science. Science operates on the basis of empirical research and probabilities, not opinions. A therapist is to help a patient rise above the expressions of popular points of view, the opinions of famous people such as "pop" stars, or the field of what is known as "pop" psychology. Patients deserve from the therapist the best of current knowledge based on the best of empirical research strategies.

MY COMMENT: The therapist needs to reduce and resolve any controversy, not contribute to it.

12.
THERAPISTS CAN HANDLE EMBARRASSING SITUATIONS THAT MAY ARISE

In the course of my clinical practice, I have occasionally been confronted or placed in a situation of temptation, the old-fashioned kind. Old-fashioned in the sense that it has been a part of the human dilemma for thousands of years. The most notable historical figure was that of Joseph and Potiphar's wife. Thankfully, I have not been in that type of blatant situation, but subtle forms of enticement can be just as powerful.

Thankfully, early in my clinical career. I was reminded years ago of the decision by Billy Graham to never be alone with a woman. This was reinforced when I visited the office of an attorney who told me of the policy of that office. The policy was clear and resounding – never be in the same room alone with a woman.

Throughout my fifty years of practice, I can greatly attest to the fact that such temptation and potential downfall has not been my experience. I am grateful that my clinical practice has always included the hiring of a female office support team, along with my wife serving as my office bookkeeper. Over the years, this arrangement has added unmeasured safety and support for me and my patients.

Temptation bites, but it does not need to impair or destroy. Acting on temptation viciously destroys and impairs the therapist and the practice of psychology of the therapist. One is never the same and the practice is never the same. In fact, my advice for a therapist who has overstepped the line under such situations is, terminate the practice, leave the profession, and go get a new life and career. Values and priorities also need to be put back in order. For patients, I recommend that they seek another therapist, but continue their search for wholeness.

MY COMMENT: The "lone wolf" therapist is vulnerable and at risk. A group practice offers certain protections for both the therapist and the patient.

13.
PHOTOS OF THE THERAPIST'S FAMILY ON DISPLAY CAN ENCOURAGE PROGRESS

I recall during my years of training that I was advised to not place photos of my family in my therapy office. The rationale was that photos of my family might make patients either jealous or aggravate areas of pain in their life. Interestingly, I never heard any discussion or research as to the relative advantages and disadvantages of having a family photo in my office visible to patients as they come and go.

Over the years, I have developed a practice and indeed include family pictures in my office. I did not make them particularly conspicuous, however. Actually, I have found that family photos generate discussion and allows me to introduce therapeutic topics on family life and of the family life of the patient. Yes, it may be important to not place family photos in a situation where it might be seen as either competitive or braggadocios.

I keep them inconspicuous. I keep them simple. I keep all photos modest and positive and constructive. If the topic ever comes up and is discussed or referenced during a session, I don't make my family the focus of discussion or set up a competitive focus. I try to keep the focus on the patient's own family and its role in their life. I try to help the patient use the photo and discussion as a way to build their own family life better.

MY COMMENT: A therapist has a family and should be proud of them as an example of a healthy family life.

14.
DEALING WITH THREATS IS NECESSARY
THE THERAPIST AND THE PATIENT

While it is not very common, therapists do experience threats from patients. I have had one threat in my fifty years of practice. However, recently I had a situation which yielded a moderate possibility of a threat coming my way. Of course, patients sometimes do not like what you say, issues you raise, or discussions that involve very delicate and difficult events and circumstances in their life. It is uncommon, but every once in a while a patient cannot handle certain discussion points and see it as an attack and then counter that attack with a threat against you as a therapist. This is even more true today, unfortunately, than when I started my practice fifty years ago.

My most blatant experience was over 38 years ago when a young girl, older than 16, came to me for counseling without the knowledge of her parents. The law allows for that under certain circumstances, abuse being one of them. She came to divulge the fact that her father had molested her and she could not confront him or tell anyone for fear that he would learn about it and then retaliate against her and her mother.

Once hearing about the abuse, by law I am obligated to report this to law enforcement. I called Child Protective Services. They in turn with the police contacted the father and apprised him of the accusation and began an investigation into the claim.

The father went ballistic. He called my office and indicated that he was coming down within the hour and that he had a gun and was going to even the score with me. Now that's a real threat!

I proceeded to take protection action. I closed the office, locked the doors, and sent the secretaries home. I went to an undisclosed location and called the police regarding this threat to make it a part of their investigation, and to provide protection for me.

Thankfully, it was diffused and we heard nothing further.

Every therapist must be trained and be prepared to act in such situations when personal attack comes their way. It is a matter of decisive action, quick action, and protective action for oneself and for others.

While being prepared to protect oneself, it is also essential that a therapist act to protect patients, staff, and anyone in the area at the time. It is imperative that patients and all others not only feel safe, but are safe while in the office of a therapist.

MY COMMENT: Take threats seriously and know how to protect those in your charge, as well as yourself.

15.
SORTING OUT ADVICE GIVEN BY OTHER THERAPISTS AND FRIENDS MAY BE NECESSARY

It's not uncommon for a patient during therapy to quote a prior therapist they have consulted or state a quotation from some special friend or family member regarding some point of interest or concern related to their problem for which therapy is being sought. How do I deal with that? How does any therapist deal with advice coming to a patient from another therapist? How to express a different opinion from another therapist and yet make the best out of the patient's experiences with a prior therapist?

Even if I disagree with another therapist, it is generally my policy to acknowledge the quote and try to use it favorably as I can. It is important to understand and keep the focus on the patient's concerns, problems, issues, and the goals that are of focus in the therapy. After acknowledging the quote and trying to utilize it in a constructive way, I then try to alter the quote in a way that is more in keeping with the goals I'm trying to achieve and the issues I am trying to advance with the patient. In other words, I try to use that or any quote from another person for good.

Further, I then try to build on the quote and put it in my own terms or change it completely. I then try to give an alternative quote or a quote that is more relevant and helpful to the patient as I see them now in their life and the issues they have shared with me, as their current therapist.

The prior therapist meant well, I am sure, even if he/she were off the track. Perhaps it was a meaningful quote at that time in the patient's life, but it is now different.

MY COMMENT: Consider the source, as advice can be cheap.

16.
THERAPISTS ALSO EDUCATE THEIR COMMUNITY THROUGH TV INTERVIEWS AND POD CASTS

Today a local television station called and asked if they could come to the office and interview me on a particular criminal activity which recently took place in our community. They wanted me to discuss the psychological aspects of community-based crime.

I always try to accommodate the media when they call. Not only does it give opportunity for my services to be better known to the community, but it also gives a great opportunity to educate the community on mental health and psychological matters. It is important for me to assist in the healing process when tragedy strikes, weather the tragedy is personal or community based.

The news topic today was on a teenage criminal spree that is going on in our community. I not only addressed the issue of the criminal behavior, but also spoke of ways in which parents need to step up to the plate and become more responsible in monitoring their children's whereabouts and social behavior. Thereby protect our community. I was able to strongly emphasize the role of the parent as a protector of the community. To do so, they need to be very much aware of what their children are doing and with whom they are engaged outside of the home.

Therapists have a unique role when they are interviewed by the media on current events which capture the attention of the general community. This is part of my commitment which I have maintained throughout my entire professional career. I believe in "giving psychology away." Who is better to receive my advice and guidance than my community?

MY COMMENT: Give psychology away as others need it, but may not realize it.

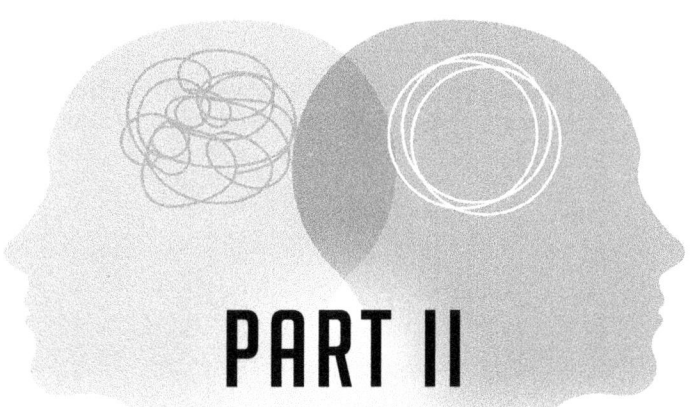

PART II

CAN THERAPY HELP ME DEAL WITH MY PROBLEMS?

17.
DURING STRESSFUL TIMES, HELP IS APPRECIATED

In my session with Lewis today, a patient with chronic pain, we spoke of the few people who give him encouragement. We then spoke of the people who have been discouraging and not particularly helpful. Interestingly, they were all a part of his friendship circle.

The comments caused me to reflect on the old adage that "misery loves company." Actually, as I told Lewis, this is not a true adage. What is true, however, is that, "Misery loves miserable company." It's not only important and necessary that we have people in our life when we are experiencing misery, but we want and need people in our life who understand our misery because they have gone through it themselves, or are in the process of going through it themselves.

In other words, there is an unspoken understanding and support that exists between those going through a common stressful experience. What is important to know is that we get general support from others, but primary support comes from those who have a common sense of empathy, a common sense of understanding, and a common sense of shared experience. This is because they have already processed, experienced, and know the story and the pathway that Lewis and others are now experiencing and living out.

It is only then that we really feel understood, accepted, and embraced. It is only then do we experience the healing power that comes from one's personal support system.

MY COMMENT: When hurting, seek out those who really understand you because they are or have been in the same boat as you.

18.
THE HEALING PROCESS AFTER TRAUMA

Today, I spoke with Joel who is now processing the trauma of a tragic accident in which his beloved father was fatally injured. To make matters worse, the car in which the father was driving was struck by a police officer on a call and driving above the speed limit at the time.

In helping Joel process this event, we spoke about the father's life and his influence on Joel from childhood until the present time. It was generally a very warm and loving relationship over time. We then devoted talk time to his experiences and feelings towards police officers before the accident and since the accident. We also spoke of his experience with previous accidents and how the police handled the matter at the time.

In other words, it was a quagmire of issues to be sorted out. That is why therapy is so important. Such complex resolution of issues cannot be processed and figured out alone. Nor can it be done with unprofessional and untrained people with whom one might speak.

It's only as you sort out the issues that you can then identify emotions attached to the various issues and how those various emotions can be modified, moderated, and eventually resolved so they don't linger and cause additional hurt over time.

Anytime one is going through trauma, it's important to get involved with a psychologist who is uniquely trained to not only understand trauma but can sort out the factors in a healthy manner. Don't go about trying to resolve trauma alone. You need supportive friends and a professional who has a listening ear and an interactive and problem-solving style in therapy.

MY COMMENT: Resolve trauma one part or issue at a time with the help of friends and a therapist.

19.
SUPPORT ANIMALS CAN BE HELPFUL IN COPING WITH ANXIETY

Support animal present during the therapy session has become increasingly more common. Many more patients want to bring their support animal with them. For some it is to merely show me their animal, and for others, it is a state of anxiety being calmed by the presence of their support animal.

Support animals are of all sizes and shapes: fish, dogs, cats, wolves, to name a few.

I was caused to consider this issue more seriously yesterday when a patient I was seeing for the first time came with an extremely large, bold, and mean-looking pitbull. Pitbulls scare me. I view them as being unpredictable and vicious. I have treated many patients who have been attacked and seriously bitten by pitbulls. So, now when I have a pitbull join in on a therapy session with a patient, it is a time of increased anxiety for me.

I can understand the role support and service animals play in the lives of many individuals. This particular pitbull was indeed a support animal for this gentleman who was a 7-year veteran from Iraq with serious and debilitating symptoms of Post-Trauma Stress Disorder related to the military and his time in Iraq. Indeed, he needed a support animal.

A support animal can be helpful by being involved and given a role to play in the therapy program from the start. Consider the following:

1. As a therapist, I must not manifest any fear of the animal, but an acceptance as would any family member of my patient.

2. The support animal provides opportunity for me to build a bridge of trust with the patient.

3. As I come to accept the animal, I also give indication of acceptance of the person, as well.

4. Therapy can include the support animal by giving a role for the animal to play in the life of the patient during therapy.

5. There are always topics that are difficult to discuss, but would be more easily discussed if an assignment was given to the patient to talk to the support animal first and then come to therapy ready to discuss the issue or the topic.

6. A dog coming regularly to therapy can be used to assess progress. If the patient is less reliant on the dog over time, progress is assumed to have taken place. If the dog is given more freedom to be on his own and the patient needing to be less controlling of the animal, progress can be assumed.

7. Is it notable that the patient interacts differently with the animal once therapy has sufficiently progressed? It is also important to note if the animal is being treated with greater care and greater kindness and softness, and the interactive is less controlling and authoritarian. Then progress can be assumed.

Finally, it might be a reasonable goal for the patient to come to therapy without the support animal and be able to go about the community more freely without the presence of the support animal all the time.

These same ways of incorporating an animal in therapy can be used in the home. Any animal can be an opportunity to teach new behaviors and to assess progress on the part of a child or adult in such behavior patterns as kindness, responsibility, caring, and courage.

MY COMMENT: Support animals are vital to some people, but a total dependance on them is not healthy.

20.
HEALING OF A BRAIN INJURY

My session today with an older gentleman, who had experienced a recent motor vehicle accident, was critical to his recovery. In the accident, he was rear-ended and suffered a whiplash injury and a significant trauma.

Whiplash injuries are well-known to have a concussion effect on the brain as a result of the brain being jostled within the head at the time of impact. It is not uncommon to experience injury to the back of the brain, as well as in the forebrain, when one is rear-ended in an accident. This was the case with this gentleman.

The brain injury occurs when the head goes forward and then snaps back and the brain is caused to tear way from the skin holding it in place in the front and back when it is jostled about at the time of impact. This is called "searing." Unfortunately, the injury to the brain can cause lasting damage or at least long-term damage. For example, it might be more difficult to process information thereafter. Confusion and tiredness are common affects from such accidents.

One of the primary strategies for healing the brain is sleep. It is important to get a good night's sleep after such an injury, even an extra hour or two.

It is also important to take a mid-day nap of one hour. With such a brain injury, it is common to feel tired or exhausted mid-day. Hence, a one-hour mid-day nap is not only helpful from the point of view of restoring the brain from the injury, but also to facilitate the healing process from the emotional trauma of the accident.

There are other healing exercises, several of which I reviewed with him. As we discussed his best options, I recommended walking, memory exercises, balance exercises, and the use of medication. He found these recovery activities to be workable and something he could plan for in his daily schedule.

MY COMMENT: Sleep is healing for those who have experienced trauma, high stress events, or a brain injury, to name a few.

21.
ABANDONMENT, NEGLECT, AND REJECTION OF A CHILD

It is all too common to interview or evaluate people who claim they have been abandoned at some point in their life. They usually point to the time their parents divorced, the time when a parent suddenly leaves the home, the time that they had a tragic death in the family, or when the family moved during a critical time frame.

To be sure, abandonment is one of the most hurtful and defeating events that children can experience. And, it is an experience for which they are not prepared and with which they are unable to cope.

I think there is another factor that operates in the lives of many children. That is rejection. Many kids have not been abandoned, but certainly have been rejected. Rejection can be emotional rejection, and or, physical rejection. Rejection usually occurs at the time of birth when a mother does not accept her child or turns her child over to another person such as grandparents, the father, or an adoptive family to raise.

Abandonment is very different from rejection. Many children are rejected in that they were never taken in, accepted, loved, or taught to believe there is a positive future. These are the rejected kids. Many of them find their way into the welfare and foster home environment to be forgotten.

On the other hand, an abandoned child is one that has been taken in and given a sense of identify and a sense of future and hope, but then having that hope dashed by a parent's loss of interest, loss of commitment, loss of involvement, or loss of connection. This may happen at a time of a divorce. For example, all children going through the divorce of their parents feel abandoned. The parents spend more time fighting with each other, pursuing other interests, developing a new life, reorganizing their life, or just surviving on their own. The child in such situations often become a secondary concern.

A child can also be abandoned at the time of a death or major trauma or physical impairment of a parent which renders them unable to provide the loving support and connection they have had with their child up until now.

Further, a child also can be abandoned at a time when the parents go through a major trauma or change in their life such as change of employment, change of economic status, or change of location such as moving. In other words, whenever a parent becomes preoccupied with other major events, children feel abandoned and experience a major loss of attention and involvement with their parents.

A child can also be abandoned at a time when the parent changes their lifestyle, such as becoming drug-oriented and establishes a life of some addiction. This leads to the parent becoming emotionally bland and disinterested in the life and welfare of the child.

Further, a child can be neglected when a parent is available but preoccupied and lacks the necessary actions to relate to and interact with the child. This child is generally seen as a necessary evil and "in the way."

This was the case of Robert who told me at great lengths about his early years in which he was abused and abandoned. He was shifted from "pillar to post" and had no stability until his late teens. The feeling of being accepted and appreciated has been an unsolved issue in his life ever since.

Long term therapy is anticipated as he deals with these problem issues for the rest of his life like so many others must do.

MY COMMENT: Parents, be steadfast, involved and committed.

22.
THE PAIN AND SORROW OF PTSD

Today, I met with Joel, a veteran, with many years of military experience and now on a disability discharge due to having Post Trauma Stress Disorder (PTSD). At times, he is a basket case. At times, he functions well. The question that I perused in therapy with him was, "What makes the difference? How can somebody with a mental or cognitive disorder be normal and appear regular at one time and then be very disabled and dysfunctional at another?" That led to our having a lengthy discussion over several sessions about his PTSD and how it came about.

PTSD is a complex problem calling for a specialized approach in treatment. It usually requires several components to a treatment plan. Accordingly, my therapy approach with such individuals is divided into several components, such as the following issues:

1. Separating out any exposure to news which is military-oriented from that which is civilian-oriented. The goal is to avoid and remove oneself from military thinking and experiences and only become enmeshed in civilian futuristic ideas, images, and experiences.

2. Stop watching militaristic news broadcasts but rather focus on television programs which are non-conflictual, and non-authoritarian in purpose.

3. Do not work for an employer or in a work environment which is militaristic such as the military, law enforcement, the post office, governmental agencies, the IRS, and security companies.

4. Seek out employment which is family-oriented, friendship-oriented, and where you can work independently. Get into farming or some such non-conflict work and avoid high-conflict employment such as law enforcement.

5. Read and talk to people not associated with the military life. Focus on relationships and individuals who have not been in a

hierarchical or militaristic occupation and lifestyle, and thus do not think that way.

6. Learn thought-stopping and thought-management strategies.

MY COMMENT: If trauma is your story, stay clear of any reminders or components of the trauma. You don't need to be reliving the trauma daily if you can avoid it.

23.
DEALING WITH PAIN CONSTRUCTIVELY

As part of my practice, I evaluate individuals for insurance companies with chronic pain to determination if the patient is likely to benefit from surgery or some other type of pain management medical procedure. In evaluating patients who live with pain for 5, 10, 20 years or more, it is very interesting to engage them in discussion about how people respond to them and try to be of help to them in managing their pain.

Most patients indicate that chronic pain promotes compassion on the part of family members, friends, and even those in the medical profession whom they consult. However, such interest and support usually last for a time. Unfortunately, those who claim to be interested in being a support person only last for a short time period. Unfortunately, some pain patients come to enjoy the extra attention but it helps maintain the pain level. Unfortunately, in the pursuit of more attention.

Now compassion is separate from sympathy and it is different from interested concern. Compassion involves an investment of energy and an investment of time by others for a patient who carries the daily burden of pain.

Compassion has a healing component, a caring component, and an empathetic component. It brings people together. It helps connect. It helps the pain patient feel of value.

In contrast, sympathy perpetuates the pain and the need for it. It is not a healing pattern in a relationship. Short term and brief sympathy are fine, but should not be long term.

Any and all responses and actions from others for a pain patient should be based on progress and action steps to address the pain constructively to promote healing.

MY COMMENT: Pain is real, but can be altered and aggravated by the way people respond when you complain of pain.

24.
CAN TATTOOS AND PIERCING ALLEVIATE STRESS?

My secretary brought up the topic of having a tattoo. She did so half-jokingly. I commented that for my staff, as well as for anyone, the display of tattoos is a choice of having a job or not, or having a particular job or not. Every employer has a policy and preference relative to their staff being adorned with tattoos. Before getting a tattoo one needs to weigh the options, benefits, and the consequences, both short term and long term, particularly in regards to employment.

Tattoos have been with us for hundreds of years. However, what is being done today, particularly among our youthful members of society, is an exercise in self-esteem enhancement and trying to compensate or overcome one's bodily dysphoria. Having tattoos is a dysfunctional method or way of trying to correct something that is perceived as incorrect, inadequate, or undesirable. To be sure, tattoos are no way to cover up one's own personal inadequacy, protect oneself from fearful people, or to create some kind of personal enhancement or bodily advantage over somebody else.

True personal development and acceptance comes from within as you try to become the person you were meant to be. It is inner beauty that prevails in the long run, not external beauty.

Self-acceptance is essential and basic to positive mental health. We are who we are. We were created and came forth from the womb as we are. Of major significance is learning to accept and live effectively compared to trying to create an alternative image or self-identification. Real change and lasting change must come from within and manifest in daily living patterns. Adding on some form of adornment can be an exercise in futility. Long term inner peace does not come with artistic add-ons. Long lasting peace comes from acknowledging who you are, not what you look like.

It has been asked by many, why do people who like themselves have tattoos? A good question as it hits the heart of so many people. For many it is a sign of covering up and being protected. For others, it is an anxiety reducer, and for others it is an attention getter. And even for some people it is a way to feel powerful and strong. There is no one reason or purpose for tattoos. But they do have a purpose for each person which is often sub-conscious and sub-liminal.

The use of a tattoo is merely a temporary and plastic effort to cover up deeper feelings of fear and inadequacy. Disillusionment will come. What will be required to counter each person's disillusionment? It is a vivacious cycle.

The role of parents, teachers, and other leaders of youth is to help a young person be self-accepting, live with what resources one has from birth, develop the personal skills and resources that will strengthen and enhance a person's level of success, achievement, and accomplishment in life.

MY COMMENT: Be real. Be who you are. Develop your natural skill-set, and consistently Improve yourself from within.

25.
MAKING SENSE OUT OF FEARFUL TIMES AND EVENTS

Today, I talked with a young gentleman who made a serious attempt of suicide several years ago. He vowed that he would never reach the age of 24. He now comes to his dreaded birthday, age 24. It's a painful day for him. It's a day he is reminded of a very painful event and a painful time in his life. He asks, "How do I change that memory? How do I deal with the embarrassment and fear?"

In the course of my discussion, we developed a plan in which the year "24", his birthday year, would be dealt with in a constructive way by doing opposite events. Up to now, age 24 was feared and dreaded. It was a painful time to which to look forward. So, I said, okay, let's look at "24" and make it into some positive experiences, such as the loss of 24 pounds, a walk of 24 miles, a gathering of 24 friends, a plan of 24 events over the next year, and the list went on. He grabbed ahold of the idea. It gave him a different perspective on how to anticipate the day of his birthday and put it into a more constructive and positive theme. It became a time to anticipate and look forward to instead of something to regret and be ashamed of for years to come.

To do the opposite of that which you fear is a behavioral principle for change. Unfortunately, when we have fear we avoid a particular time, event, person, or situation and then live to regret it. On the other hand, it's better to find the alternative. It is also a good thing to find the opposite and set a new direction for life by which to thrive.

MY COMMENT: When feeling fearful or regretting something, do the opposite. Face your fear and change it.

26.
STUTTERING IS ESSENTIALLY A PROBLEM OF HEARING

Kyle was obviously a stutterer. From the very first sentence in our first session together, words came out in a staccato, uneven fashion. Dysfluency was demonstrated throughout the session. With patience, I listened to his concerns for which he came for counseling. With empathy, I tried to console and reassure him that he was safe and should feel at ease.

At the end of the session, I commented about his being a stutterer and that I too was a stutterer. Growing up as a stutterer, I understand very much what he was experiencing and what life is like for him. I then indicated that I would like to spend a little time in the next session teaching him how not to stutter. Kyle showed interest. We agreed.

During our second session, I again introduced the issue of his stuttering and that he could learn to become more fluent and create a greater sense of confidence as he improved his flow of speech. As a result, his relationships would expand, as would his daily social experience.

First, I introduced the idea that stuttering is not a <u>speech</u> problem but a <u>hearing</u> problem. I explained that as you speak, sound waves go out into the air and then come around and enter the ear. You then process auditorily what you just said verbally. You also have sound waves within the mouth that go into the inner ear and you process again the sounds from inside the mouth just as you do the external sounds.

However, in a stutterer, there is a disconnect or dysfluency between the speed of speaking and the speed of hearing. Stutterers hear or process sounds more slowly than they speak. For those that have fluent speech, there is a coordination between the speed of speaking and the speed of hearing and the processing of it. It is this disconnection or incoordination that creates the unevenness of speech and the dysfluency of the flow of the speech. It is called Delayed Auditory Feedback.

Secondly, I introduced the idea that it is important to learn to speak more slowly so that your speed of speech can be balanced and coordinated with your speed of hearing. Just by slowing down, one can speak more fluently because there is a better coordination between speed of hearing and the slower speed of speech.

Thirdly, Kyle had to learn that the speed of his speech had to coordinates with the speed of his hearing. For some, it is very slow so they have to speak very slowly. For others, they can speak a little bit more rapidly, but cannot speak too rapidly because they then experience the incoordination again between speed of speech and speed of hearing. Each stutterer must find his or her own speed of speech to match his or her speed of hearing. It is a very personal and individualized process.

Finally, I told Kyle, it is essential that he begin to speak slowly every day in all situations. It takes practice and practice, like anything else. By consistently speaking slowly, he would learn to speak without stuttering or speak with much less of it. It is a lifetime commitment of speaking slowly. One must consistently monitor his own speaking pace and keep it in the comfort zone of speaking.

MY COMMENT It is better to speak slowly and be understood, than not at all, or in an uncoordinated and dysfluent manner.

27.
BODILY INJURY LEADS TO A LOSS OF INDEPENDENCE

Recently, I met with a lady who injured her hand in a work-related accident to the point that she lost feeling and coordination and movement of the hand. The medical opinion indicated that the loss of the function of the hand was permanent and that she would have to learn to cope with it. In all likelihood, as a music professor, she would need to seek a new occupation and profession. Hence, she came to therapy so that we could together give consideration to this very significant injury and change in her life.

Our discussed caused me to reflect on our hands and their psychological significance. Sure, hands allow us to perform various functions, occupationally, domestically, and in many other ways. Our hands allow independence and facilitate achievement in many areas of life.

Psychologically, hands allow us to comfort others, support others, and be of encouragement to others, such as a pat on the back, a squeeze of the hand, or just a light touch on the arm.

Hands also give us a sense of independence. It is with our hand that we are able to carry out various tasks and do things for ourselves rather than to rely on others.

Hands also represent power and strength. Many tasks that we do throughout the day require the strength of a hand squeeze or the ability to carry and hold considerable weight. In so doing, we are able to accomplish a task and be independent.

Hands also represent and allow us to experience tenderness such as the holding of an infant child. The stroking of the hair as in an expression of love and consolation.

As for my patient, she had to change occupations and find new interests, and hobbies. She had to learn to live with an impairment. She had to learn how to live a new goal-directed life.

As her therapy continued over several months, she began the slow process of reorganizing her life and to live beyond the injury and its associated trauma.

MY COMMENT: Hands allow us to do everyday tasks, but are also instruments of kindness, compassion, support, love, care, and comfort. Use them well.

28.
ADULT HYPERACTIVITY CAN BE MANAGED

Recently, a local physician referred one of his 26-year-old patients for evaluation relative to the possibility of an attention disorder with hyperactivity. I met with him today and, indeed, noted from the very first five minutes of the interview that he did represent the diagnostic profile of hyperactivity with impulsivity.

In the course of my interview with him, he spoke at rapid fire pace, almost too fast for me to even follow. I immediately asked him to slow down and explained to him that he has to monitor his speed of speech to balance with his speed of hearing. If he speaks faster than he hears, he will stutter. Indeed, this was his experience as a child as he was known as a relatively severe stutterer. He continues to be a stutterer but not quite as severe at this time since he slowed down his speech a little.

Secondly, I advised him to be very much aware of the speed of which his body operates, heart rate, speed of walking, speed of eating, speed of drinking, speed of talking, and even his speed of hearing. Speed of hearing relates to the processing of information auditorily presented. We then practiced kind of a slower motion of his presentation for the rest of the session. This was difficult for him, as he was engrained for 26 years of speed talking, speed living.

We then discussed the possibility of his taking appropriate medication for hyperactivity, so I indicated that I would be in contact and coordinate that with his physician. He was very willing to cooperate.

Follow-up therapy sessions were also scheduled as he needs to have practice and time to study the differential between his normal speed of activity such as speaking and moving about and doing so at a much slower or more deliberate pace. Thankfully, he was open to this suggestion. We decided to proceed accordingly.

It is important to note that no child or adult should be given medication for attention-deficit or for hyperactivity by itself. Medication may be helpful, and it usually is in most cases, but it must be used in coordination with and in conjunction with a personal therapy program and family therapy. Usually, 5 to 9 sessions are needed. Thankfully, he was open to this recommendation and arrangement.

It is important to note that the family physician was cooperative and handled the medication component of his treatment plan. Good results came from this coordinated effort.

MY COMMENT: Slowing down is often a significant help to many patients who experience processing problems.

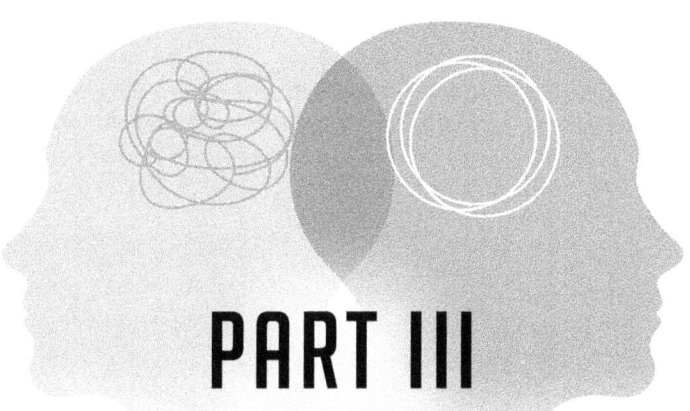

PART III

CAN THERAPY HELP ME OVERCOME DISCOURAGEMENT?

29.
STRENGTHENING SELF-ESTEEM HELPS OVERCOME DISCOURAGEMENT

Mary was no exception of low self-esteem.. In fact, there are many "Marys" in this world. Mary represents those who live daily with a profound feeling and sense of low self-esteem. They are not sure of their worth, their value, their importance, their acceptance, and their impact upon others in the world in which they live. Mary, like others, lived in doubt, uncertainty, unsureness, and tentativeness in all areas of her life. She asked, can I help her?

As it is my usual practice when discussing this topic, I spoke of self-esteem as being a figment of one's imagination and erroneous self-belief, as compared to it being a reality or something of positive and true substance. I spoke of self-esteem as being an irrational feeling or impression. I also spoke of self-esteem as being temporal and that it changes over time and from one situation to another. Not only does self-esteem change over time, but it changes within the social context of those with whom one relates at any given time. There are times when your relationships give you a sense of value and there are other times when your relationships contribute to a sense of self-devaluation. These are two states with which we struggle all our lives.

Further, one's self-esteem is learned like any other behavior pattern. Each time we say something about our-self, we either affirm ourself, derive affirmation about what we just said from others, or react negatively. Any behavior or statement we make is reinforced positively or negatively. All positively rewarded statements are retained and become our self-reference. Negative manners result in negative self-esteem.

For the person struggling with low self-esteem, such discussion may come across as academic. It doesn't pack much of an encouraging punch. It sounds more like a prerecorded lecture. What someone wants when they're feeling a sense of low self-esteem is reassurance of their value and sense of acceptance. It's like a cup of instant coffee. They want it now, they want it without any particular degree of effort, and they want it served to them by someone important and of high value in their life.

Self-esteem also comes from the long-term commitments and support of family and friends. Positive relationships have a positive impact on us. Self-esteem also comes from a lifetime of personal expansion such as trying new things and exposing oneself to new people and new situations. Essentially, self-esteem comes from one's own problem- solving effort and daily determination to live better. It is not something that someone can give you, although we would like it to be that way. To be sure, it is earned the old-fashion way, one day at a time. We all learn it the same way.

Here are four points that I shared with Mary over three sessions which she found most helpful and encouraging.

1. Do something simple each morning so you will feel like you have value and that you accomplished something. Make your bed. Commend yourself for it.

2. Be around people who have positive self-esteem and learn from them. Observe them, listen to them, imitate them, do what they do, speak as they speak, and reference yourself as they reference themselves.

3. Learn to be self-rewarding, self-reinforcing. Whenever you do something that is better than you did before or that went reasonably well, commend yourself, praise yourself, and reward yourself in the same way for your improvement.

4. Deliberately do something each day, or at least each week that puts you in a situation with new people, new experiences, and new opportunities so that life situations and events give you a good feeling of yourself as you enter in the world of daily positive experiences.

MY COMMENT: Be proactive and positive in your social contacts; notice how you are just as good as anyone else. Praise yourself for any and all positive actions and interactions with others.

30.
GRATITUDE HELPS MANAGE DISCOURAGEMENT

During my counseling with a young couple, I was caused to focus on their history of ungratefulness and encourage them to show more gratitude and thanksgiving to each other and for each other.

To be sure, this was a huge missing component in their relationship as it is in our world today. There is a profound lack of gratitude today, especially among our youth. We are a world of taking, but little gratitude is expressed in the process. Somehow we have missed the point. We are not teaching our young people today to express thankfulness and gratefulness for what they have, what they are given, and the opportunities provided them within their home, school, church, and general community.

It should be noted that generous people are content with whatever financial circumstances they have. Generous people give liberally to charity whether they have a lot or have very little. They give because they are content in themselves. Generosity is a heart issue, not a pocketbook issue.

Further, consumer debt ultimately comes from lack of contentment and satisfaction in our lives. It has been said, "Debt comes from wanting more than God's current provision for our life and arranging other ways to get it."

It all begins with a lack of contentment. Maybe you just graduated from school; or you watched friends move into new homes and buy newer cars. Instead of living simply and tackling your debt – being content and patient with your current provision level – you make decisions that lead you into a kind of slavery. Essentially, you are saying, "I messed up my provision level. I need more money now." It might feel good for a moment, but debt puts us in bondage to a lender.

In the process of our three sessions together, I encouraged this young couple to begin a gratitude journal in which they would record daily something for which they are grateful. They were to do this for an entire week and at the end of each week they were to share with each other what they had written down during the week.

This activity was designed to help them begin to be aware of things for which to be grateful and to begin the process of expressing it in written as well as verbal form. Ultimately, my goal was to help them become more verbally expressive of gratitude and thankfulness for each other and for the things each of them contributed to the relationship on a daily basis.

As this couple undertook this assignment, their relationship began to show encouraging signs of wellness and personal enjoyment with each other. Indeed, gratitude again demonstrated its powerful and healing influence in a relationship.

From session to session, I kept reminding this couple of the positive benefits that come from being grateful and expressing it openly and regularly.

> **MY COMMENT:** Seeds of discouragement cannot take root in a heart that is grateful.

31.
USING CREATIVE WRITING AS AN ENCOURAGING PROCESS

Today, I happened to meet with two young men about three hours apart from each other – one in the morning and one in the afternoon. Both of them were budding artists. One was writing music and the other was writing poetry. Both were discouraged about their progress and both felt stuck.

In speaking with them, we spoke about a way in which ideas are generated and later converted into music or into a poem. We also talked about ways in which they are encouraged or discouraged by other people in their writing process. We considered the purpose of their writing and creativity. We reflected on their long-term potential. These issues were essential to understand why and how they were stuck, so I could be of help to them.

While they didn't know each other and probably never will, they both shared a degree of freshness and excitement when talking about their writing. Otherwise, there was a mood of depression that prevailed. It was the depression that really was the purpose for which they came for therapy week after week.

It's been said, and to some degree this is true, people who are creative and artistic often have a prevailing degree of mild depression. The depression is usually not intense or debilitating, but enough to interfere with the process of one's life. We call low grade, chronic depression with which people live, but function, Dysthymia.

I would say that both of these young gentlemen were displaying dysthymia as a primary mood and both needed to learn how to live with it. They either had to learn to overcome dysthymia and live above it, or learn to live with it and not let it become debilitating. Dysthymia is not impairing but it is living life while carrying a heavy load. A moderately heavy load, to be sure.

Interestingly, and predictively, as their dysthymia improved over time, by being less sullen, so did their creative writing. They both reported that they were beginning to feel like they could accomplish something again. They were beginning to be successful again. They were noticed by others again. They felt important again. And, they believed they could accomplish something once again. Speaking out and writing during therapy will overcome dysthymia and discouragement any time.

MY COMMENT: Use your skills to combat unwanted emotions.

32.
GUARDING YOUR PEACE TO COUNTER DISCOURAGEMENT

One frequent theme in therapy with men and women, boys and girls, is their perception of peace and protecting it. It is surprising how many people experience in their relationships the taking away of their peace by another person. It can be traumatic, but certainly discouraging.

This topic or piece of advice should have been taught and learned by a number of different segments of our population. For example, any child that has been bullied should have been taught the meaning of the phrase, "do not let anyone take your peace away." They also should have been taught to act upon it. For kids who were being bullied, this would have stopped the bully behavior and all the trauma associated with it.

Likewise, this phrase should have been learned by every woman who has been abused by a powerful and demeaning man or woman in their life. This would have either stopped the abusive behavior or given the woman the determination to stand up for herself and resist being abused.

No child should be bullied and no woman should be abused. In other words, no one should be allowed to take the peace of another person away.

This is a piece of learning that every child should undertake as they start school. The lesson needs to be taught and learned in kindergarten. To have peace and know how to maintain peace is a vital task for everyone. Yes, all aspect of one's peace has to be equally recognized and honored. One's peace must be protected and guarded. It's a vital commodity.

Protecting one's peace is a lesson to be learned early in life. It's a lesson in self-protection. Social relationships and personal integrity are essential aspects of a person's life, along with keeping your peace. Protect these parts of your life vigorously.

MY COMMENT: Don't let anyone take your peace away.

33.
COMPLIMENTS HELP TO TURN THE TABLE ON DISCOURAGEMENT

Early in each therapeutic session, I look for opportunity to compliment the patient for something that has been accomplished, attempted, or engaged in outside of the patient's comfort zone. It is well-known that compliments bring people together and connect people. This is one way for me to establish a connection especially with a new patient,

I want that kind of connection with my patients as I'm sure they do with me. Compliments encourage, strengthen, and give hope: three commodities often lacking in individuals coming to therapy. It's like putting cash into somebody's pocket.

Patients come from a background of being judged all day long. They've grown up in families that judge, pre-judge, and excessively judge. Compliments have generally been in short supply. In contrast to critical comments or remarks, we all respond to words of encouragement and affirmation, two great forms of a compliment.

I often supplement a compliment during the early stages of each therapy session. For example, I keep note of and look for opportunity to express a compliment or a statement of recognition and praise to a person at critical times in their life such as sending a birthday card, or a note. People like that. They like to be recognized. In a world of people being overlooked and forgotten, it is uplifting to be recognized, included, and appreciated.

Of particular and critical timing is the untimely death of a loved one. Sending a sympathy card to recognize a family member's death and even sending a get-well card at times of serious illness are other ways to give a boost to a person's self-esteem and feeling of being cared for and not forgotten. These acts help in turning the tables on discouragement, to be sure.

However, due to confidentiality issues, it is important to be careful about how and where a card is given. It is always important to be sensitive to issues of confidentiality.

MY COMMENT: Learning how to receive and solicit compliments from others are much worthy undertakings.

34.
PRACTICING KINDNESS IS AN ANTIDOTE FOR DISCOURAGEMENT

I asked Clarice the other day, as I commonly do with single women, about her list of characteristics that she ranks most valuable regarding a hypothetical long-term, ideal partner to marry. Clarice responded pretty closely to what the research indicates on this topic. The most desirable trait in a projected mate is usually that of kindness, as it was for her.

I noted that men tend to favor physical attraction, while women favor kindness and good financial standing as being very critical to the top-of-the line selection factor. Other things important to Clarice were that of chastity, creativity, humor, physical attractiveness, and religiosity. To be sure, kindness wins out as the primary trait.

That led to a considerable amount of discussion as to her preference for kindness and her comfort level in receiving kindness from others. The session devoted to this topic was very important for her in facing the current aspect of her life and behavior patterns. She admitted to being very short on having close friendships, certainly long-term relationships. In our discussion we traced her lack of friends to her high demand for expressed kindness from others, as well as other behavior patterns as noted above.

In the following session, we held a productive discussion on the issue of "random acts of kindness" in her life. She agreed to start there. We both agreed that even random acts of kindness would get her started on a new path of "specific kindness" and be more receptive to the kind acts of others, especially men. Ultimately, she has to learn the art of kindness and apply it regularly in her give-and-take daily relationships. Kindness is expressed in words, gifts, or offering to help with a chore or task such as going grocery shopping for a neighbor or shut-in. There are countless ways to be kind and gracious towards another person as well as receive kindness from others. Again, giving and receiving kindness is learned sometimes the hard way, but it does take time and specific intent.

MY COMMENT: To learn kindness, start expressing and carrying out "random acts of kindness."

35.
OVERCOMING FEAR IS NECESSARY FOR DEFEATING DISCOURAGEMENT

Fear and anxiety have become the hallmark emotions of today's society. They are like the common cold or flu. Anxiety has increased exponentially. Fear has also become a common feeling of the future for both the young and the old. Fear of the unknown and fear of being unprotected is paramount among adults as well as our youth today.

Further, it is beyond belief what people are doing these days to reduce their anxiety and fear. Some actions are rational and some not so rational. Just how do people deal with anxiety and fear?

I met today with Jose who was expressing a considerable amount of fear as he was facing several areas of change and uncertainty within his life. They could have profound implications for the future. Three sessions were devoted to his fears, both rational and irrational fears. We had to separate them out before we could address them therapeutically. Interestingly, over the three to four sessions his level of discouragement began to dissipate. The irrational fears began to resolve and the real fears began to come under control.

We talked about the following formula for him to practice as he became less fearful and more self-managing:

FEAR

F – Face your fears

E – Expect a positive outcome

A – Assertively communicate

R – Relaxation helps reduce the tension

By applying the above formula, Jose could overcome the fear and the anxiety that otherwise would be crippling again in the future, should he ever become overwhelmed again as he was at the start of his therapy.

Fear and anxiety cannot be conquered unless one faces it directly. It must be faced in a manner that change and improvement can be expected, through a communication style that is assertive and a state of body and mind that is relaxed. When one counters fear and anxiety, discouragement fades away. It did for Jose.

MY COMMENT: When anxious, utilize the FEAR formula.

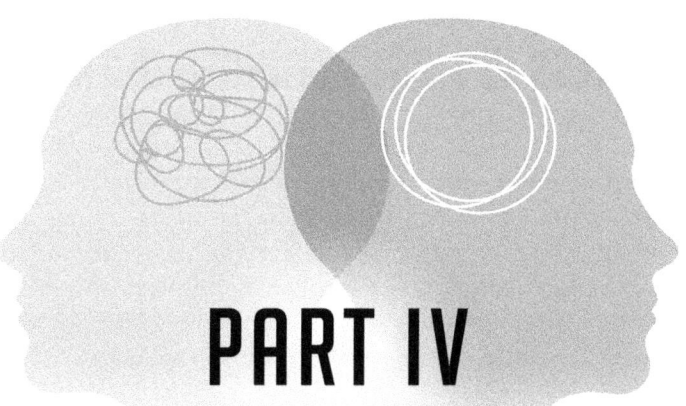

PART IV

CAN THERAPY HELP ME LIVE A HAPPIER LIFE?

ALLAN G. HEDBERG, Ph.D.

36.
HAPPINESS IS FIRST ACQUIRED IN THE HOME

Issachar is an example of a number of patients often seen in therapy because their given name has become unflattering among their peers. It is true, many parents name a child for the namesake of someone in the family, they like the sound of it, or it is a biblical or historical name. However, they often fail to give adequate consideration to its social significance to the child in the future, once school begins.

For example, I have seen patients with the name of "Pain," "Damn," "Easter," "Angel," and many other unflattering names. Unfortunately, such names can become the basis or cause of much ridicule and teasing throughout life, but especially during the junior high school years. Such teasing significantly contributes to a child's low self-esteem and embarrassment. Being the object of jokes and unkind words from their peers is common for those who have a name with double - meaning. A name can separate the child from the child's peers. It can separate the child from peer-related activities. It can put the child into a center circle of prevailing rejection, teasing, and other forms of unkindness.

This was the case of Issachar. As a therapist, I attempted to help the child accept his name, reconfigure his name, give new meaning to his name, tolerate teasing, and living above the teasing in spite of his name. We even considered a change of his name legally. All these are real possibilities and need to be explored with a child and his parents when a name is berating and embarrassing. Sometimes, it might call for the parents to ask for forgiveness and explain their reasoning at the time of the birth and the naming.

While I do not know what happened to Issachar in the long run, as he did not come back for therapy after a few sessions. At least, in my last therapy session with him, he had decided to learn to live above it. He also seemed to accept that he could go on and achieve a successful life in spite of it.

MY COMMENT: Whenever you are doing something that is permanent or long-lasting, think ahead and consider the long-term consequences.

37.
HAPPINESS CAN BE IMPROVED OVER TIME

Whenever I see a person or a couple within the middle-age range, I pause to bring to their attention the research on happiness. This was the case of Mitch and Andrea. They were age 48 and 49 respectively.

I told them of the research coming out of England which indicates that people from 132 different countries all testified to the same thing. The happiest years are the younger years and the older years. The unhappy years are the mid-age years, 45 to 60. This is true whether you're from a developed country or an undeveloped country. This is true whether you're male or female.

Thus, it is important for such a middle-age couple is to be asked to pause and consider ways in which they are dealing with their current level of happiness..

Now there are many things that can be done to counteract the age-based trend of unhappiness. It's different for every person, but the important thing is that you take charge of your own life, your own mood patterns, your own behavioral experience, and counteract the level of unhappiness that otherwise tends to prevail.

Further, it important to note that happiness does not come by external means or events, but basically by who you are, how you deal with life events, and the stage of life you're in. Take charge of the experiences of your life, and take charge of the things that counteract the natural tendency towards unhappiness especially in the middle years of life.

At the end of our therapy sessions with this middle-age couple, we again reviewed the issue of happiness. I was pleased to note that they had gone ahead and identified several ways in which they were going to attack the natural flow of unhappiness over the next ten years of their life. In other words, a person can put up with it, not deal with it, just endure it, or counteract it by a reaction pattern and experiences that you create for yourself.

MY COMMENT: There really are better days ahead. The best is yet to come.

38.
HAPPINESS IS ENHANCED THROUGH SHARING

This morning, I met with Sally who was not particularly known for her happiness. In fact, her countenance and general appearance as she came into the office was certainly not one of happiness. Sadness prevailed all over her countenance.

As I inquired into her lifestyle and the level of daily happiness she experiences, we began to uncover a long history of sadness deep within her childhood family. Her mother lived a very sad life. Her father was basically emotionally absent. There was not much contribution from him to her life. She was not encouraged at all. She was not praised for even a smile or any attempt to muster a positive emotion. The story goes on year upon year of general sadness, unhappiness, and the lack of any real affirmation and joy from others in her family.

As I refocused her attention on ways in which she can now reverse the process, since she is now an adult and no longer a dependent child, I soon realized that she didn't know even how to make herself become happy. She did not even know how to make other people happy or benefit from the happiness of other people. That led to a considerable lengthy discussion on how one generates happiness and benefits from one's happiness or the happiness of others. To her, happiness that comes from our relationships with others, especially our family, was an experience of which she knew nothing.

At the end of our first session, I wanted to leave her with something that she could remember and something that she could cling to and give her a sense of future and a hope. The possibility of changing her level of unhappiness to that of even a mild level of happiness was the challenge I left her with as we ended the first session.

I started our second session with the quote, "Happiness is like peanut butter." I said, "You can't help but get it on yourself when you spread it." Obviously, I wanted her to grasp the idea that she can smile, she can praise, she can thank, and she can give her blessing to other people. Thus, in an attempt to help someone else become happy, she can generate a level of happiness within herself.

Our next 5-6 sessions were devoted to reinforce these two principles of happiness. We practiced and practiced. She had homework assignments. She was taught how to smile. She was asked to take cell phone photos of herself in different smiling poses and keep the ones she liked. I wanted her to have a smile and feel good about it.

As you can see, I wanted her to engage in the proper behavior and as a result feel the proper emotions. It worked. After months of therapy, she began feel happier and enjoy her relationships, which, by the way, began to increase accordingly.

MY COMMENT: Start your happiness journey by sharing a happy event with others and get some of that happiness on yourself. Afterall, it's only spreadable peanut butter.

39.
INTERACTING WITH HAPPY PEOPLE INCREASES HAPPINESS

Many years ago, I read a research study by Professor Greenwood who conducted a study in which he praised and reinforced people in the course of an interview when they expressed certain words or certain thoughts or ideas. Otherwise, he would remain fairly bland throughout the interview. To reinforce the speaker, he would nod and smile approvingly or praise the use of a certain word or expression.

At the end of his experiment, he did a word-by-word content analysis of what people actually said during the interview. What he noticed was that people expressed themselves more frequently with words and with ideas that he had selectively reinforced throughout the interview. The more he praised certain words and certain thoughts and expressions, the more people used those words and expressions as they talked during the interview.

This research led Professor Greenwood to develop a pattern used in therapy in which a therapist listens for certain expressions from the patient and then reinforces those expressions, such as happiness expressions. The idea is to encourage happy statements, thereby generating more happiness feelings and talk.

There were certain words, ideas, and expressions that were ignored. Theoretically, the ignored phrases would fade away and be extinguished, or at lease said less frequently.

The idea was that if people actually express certain key words, thoughts, and ideas quite frequently they'll behave more consistently with those verbalizations. Hence, by changing the verbal statements of a person in the course of therapy, one can actually help them change behavior patterns to be more appropriate, healthy, and socially acceptable.

Further, it was suggested that people could become more socially involved and competent by using this idea of listening for certain words or expressions and then smile or nod when such words or expressions were stated. In so doing, one should experience greater social acceptance and involvement when interacting with others.

MY COMMENT: Change the way you talk and it will change the way you feel and relate to others.

40.
TOO MUCH OF A GOOD THING
CAN DETER HAPPINESS

I often find myself counseling someone, usually a woman, regarding the responsibilities she assumes for her family, extended family, friends, church, associations, and the other relationships in which she is involved. It is not uncommon to observe that she takes on many more responsibilities than she can handle, while, at the same time, performing them quite well.

However, over an extended period of time, she observes that she has become tired, overworked, and finds herself complaining that no one appreciates what she does or pitches in to help. Here anger and frustration with others grows and deepens.

As a result, she begins to notice herself becoming tired and fatigued, depressed, upset and often angry. She begins to be aware of her feelings about being used. Wanting to quit and "resign" from this position of servitude gets more and more pronounced.

After talking about how these kinds of situations develop over the period of time, we talked about ways in which she could have prevented herself from being taken advantaged of and placed in such overburdensome situations. My purpose is to help such a person put into perspective their volunteerism. In other words, some volunteerism is good; too much of it may not be good. This is true even if it is for family or loved ones.

I often include in my discussion the adage, "A little of a good thing is good. A lot of a good thing may not be good." In other words, if she can just keep into balance and perspective her level of volunteering and participating in activities, she will keep it manageable and things will go better for all.

However, when it gets out of control and she's frantically running around in circles trying to do everything for everybody else, she obviously becomes angry, upset, tired, worn out, and on the verge of quitting altogether. That is not a good thing. It is important to do your fair share and then allow others to do their fair share also. Sharing keeps one joyful and happy in their pursuits.

To be sure, there are people who will never volunteer, so you will have to confront them or create a situation to force them to volunteer. Remember, your own happiness depends on the principle, "Division of Power." Do your fair share and then wait for others to step forward to do their fair share. It actually happens more than you think.

MY COMMENT: A little of a good thing is good, but a lot of a good thing may not be good.

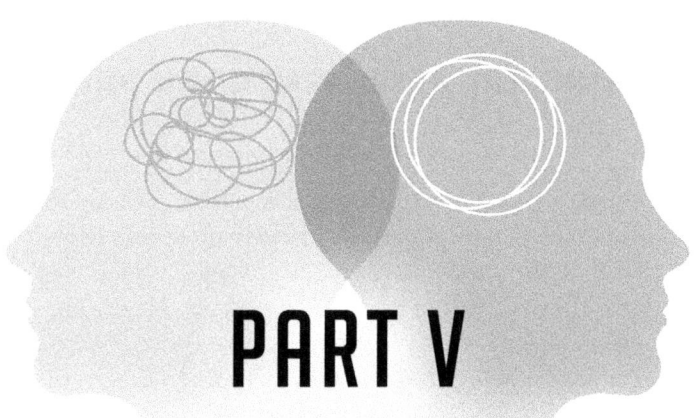

PART V

CAN THERAPY HELP ME
IMPROVE MY MARRIAGE?

41.
ADDRESS MARITAL PROBLEMS SOON AND DIRECTLY

I am amazed at the number of couples who come for marital counseling and have not read a book on marriage or even an article from a magazine. Likewise, this is a common observation among couples who are having difficulty with their children. There are many books on the market related to marriage, child management, and family life, but rarely are they read or reviewed in light of the family problems a couple is probably facing.

This was the case of Jane and Carl who have been experiencing marital difficulties for several years. When I asked what book they've consulted and how they have utilized available written materials, they sat dumbfounded. Neither of them had either bought a book or even sought out a book that might be of help to them.

In spite of their apparent non-commitment to their marriage, marital therapy commenced. We proceeded to meet over three months, weekly. Progress was noted and appreciated.

However, for Jane and Carl, as I do for many couples, I suggested a couple of book titles and how they could be obtained. Unfortunately, they never followed through with this aspect of their counseling. I also launched into two or three options that they could consider and utilize in addition to ongoing marital counseling. I proposed attending a marriage seminar or attend a marriage retreat often held in our area. As far as I know, they did not attend any seminar either.

Unfortunately, they were quite passive in addressing their marital problems.

Here are a few suggestions I shared with them:

1. Get a book and read it together at least three nights a week, reading a page or two each evening and then discussing what was read.

2. Buy a book on marriage enrichment and then read it separately, but read the same book together keeping pace with each other

so they would know what each other was reading at the time. The value of this is to give opportunity to discuss what is being read even though they're reading it separately.

3. Even if one of the couples does not read or does not have interest in reading on marital enrichment, the other should certainly do so and share what is being discussed for their mutual benefit.

4. Find a mentor to meet with them regularly during the week and more informally discuss marital issues together.

To be sure, therapy is a life event. It is an opportunity to bring together ideas, experiences, and aspirations for mutual benefit. One should not rely totally on the therapist for ideas and strategies for improvement. Therapy is a place to bring your ideas and to bring your strategies and then evaluate their relative effectiveness and benefit for you as a couple. To be sure, a therapist does have a series of ideas and recommendations and strategies that well could be utilized. However, one cannot rely upon the therapist totally. Reading sources add much benefit. This resource should be utilized as much as possible.

MY COMMENT: Successful marriages require an action plan to prevent failure and maximize the potential of a marriage.

42.
A STRESSFUL SPOUSE CAN BECOME A SOURCE OF JOY

Every once in a while, a married couple comes before me, sometimes together and sometimes separately, one of which is decidedly dysfunctional. A highly stressed or dysfunctional profile is presented, to be sure.

Dysfunctional spouses are generally from a dysfunctional family history. They live a life of addiction, are unaware of their own dysfunctional behavior, give little care as to how they affect those in their family, and live a life in pursuit of their own pleasures and self-defined happiness. Further, the dysfunctional one resists advice and instruction from others, argues with attempts to alter lifestyle, and pursues their own preferred way of having fun and seeking happiness. This is usually through the toys they buy and the free lifestyle they try to live without accountability.

Now this is a major undertaking for a therapist to address in therapy. It is easy to summarize the initial sessions with such a couple with the phrase, "divorce comes knocking."

Unfortunately, the couple whether they come separately or together, come after years of self-defeating and hurtful living making attempts of their own. Attempts on their own and through the advice of other family members, and friends and even prior therapists, have resulted in no measurable benefit.

My comment usually is along the line of "You don't need counseling to find out what your problem is because you already know. Your problem is that you don't address the issues, make the changes, and follow through to assure that the changes stick."

In other words, such couples have already been to therapy, even several times. They've already received advice from other people. They already know what their problem is. What they don't understand is how to make lasting changes that will revive, rebuild, and regenerate their marriage as well as each other. The best one can do is to reiterate what they already know from their own history and tell the couple together, "Go and sin no more." In other words, they know what to do, and they know what not to do. They don't follow up and pursue the changes they need to make and keep working on it, long term.

With such couples, I usually offer to meet three to five times to focus on the ways to identify a plan of action and follow through on the plan. This aspect of intervention is usually somewhat helpful, at least for a while.

On the other hand, I have had couples in therapy that accept my observation and agree to work on a problem area and follow through long term. Interestingly, it works.

MY COMMENT: It is not more advice, but more determination to follow through and bring about needed change based on the advice previously given.

43.
ONLINE DATING REQUIRES SPECIAL ATTENTION

Dori and Glen came for counseling just to make sure their new relationship was on solid ground and they were headed in the right direction. They met online. Nearly 4 out of 10 couples now meet online, more than any other way. This is about the 5th or 6th couple that have come to me for counseling after they met online and married. Most have been older and their second marriage following the death of a spouse.

The new marriage usually is not a problem, it's just that they want to make sure that they did the right thing and are doing well. It seems to be important to couples who marry after meeting online to be reassured they did the right thing that they're working together well, and, they will have a positive marriage. So far, my experience has been quite favorable.

Not uncommon, the adult children usually question the marriage. Much anxiety is common among the adult children of both parties. Generally, it is the female(s) in the family that have the most difficulty accepting the pending marriage. It is important to take time to answer any and all questions that represent areas of concern

In the process of counseling, three areas are usually important to be addressed. First, did we do the right thing? Second, how do we best integrate our adult children into our relationship? Third, how do we keep from comparing our current relationship to our prior marital relationship?

Once these three issues have been raised for discussion and dealt with, there is usually one more issue unique to them that remains unresolved. No two couples are the same. They each have their own unique issues to address. Adequate time needs to be provided for full discussion to take place.

In my experience, three or four sessions are needed to deal with these four issues. Thankfully, all the couples have done well as I followed them over the next year of their relationship.

> **MY COMMENT:** Computer dating is fine, but go slowly and be careful. There is no "love at first sight." It is a developmental process.

44.
DO I NEED A WILL AND TRUST?

It is my general practice when meeting with older adults to raise the question of them having a will and/or trust so that their estate is protected and their assets properly distributed according to their wishes upon their death. Nationally, only 40% of the population have a will. Fewer have a trust. I believe it is important to have a will and/or a trust if you are younger and have a child, or have assets that are fairly substantial. It is important that you determine how you want your assets distributed should you die early or when you die.

This was the case of Wilma when I met with her and she unfolded the story of her failing husband who has dementia and may have only a year or so to live. She revealed that she only had a trust, but it was twenty years old, well past the time of having a will updated. Therefore, I indicated the importance of having her trust updated, particularly in light of her husband's situation. Realizing that this is going to be a financial burden, I was able to bring to her attention resources in the community that she can consult at a reasonable cost. She was grateful for this advice and soon acted upon it.

Therapy is not only a time to change lifestyle and patterns of behavior, but also to make sure that the wishes and the future of your patient and the family are protected and preserved in accordance with their wishes and best interest. Hence, it is important to raise the question of a will and a trust.

Therapists need to be aware of many aspects of a person's life when they come for counseling, not just the initial presenting problem. That is why a wide-ranging area of discussion is needed early on in the therapy process so you understand the circumstances of the patient, the context in which they operate, and the issues they are facing in the near, as well as will be facing in the distant future.

MY COMMENT: Issues in life are not just in the here and now, but in the future of patients. Be prepared to address them in a timely manner.

ALLAN G. HEDBERG, Ph.D.

45.
FEELING THE PROPER EMOTIONS IN A MARRIAGE REQUIRES AN ACTION PLAN

Today, I had the privilege of counseling a young couple in their marriage relationship and understanding of each other. As we started the session, the husband proceeded to indicate what appeared to be a well-rehearsed statement about how he feels in the marriage. After about two or three brief statements, I interrupted him and indicated that no one really cared how he felt, because it's all based upon what he does or does not do within the context of the relationship. That brief and quick intervention surprised him but it pleased the wife.

I proceeded to indicate to him the well-stated adage, "To feel the proper emotions, one must first go through the proper motions." I then proceeded to explain the adage and how it relates to him, to his wife, and to them as a couple.

Essentially, how one feels is important but you cannot get the proper emotions by just talking about it. It is vital that you start with behavior and behave properly, and then the proper emotions will follow. The good, the desired, and the attractive emotions will follow good, desired and proper behavior.

That little discussion became a turning point in their relationship, and it helps them approached and proceeded to correct and bring about a more positive relationship with each other. For them, as it is true for so many, improved marital relationship followed over time.

MY COMMENT: Keep in mind that the desirable emotions and thoughts follow desirable behavior.

46.
DIVORCE OFTEN FOLLOWS UNRESOLVED ANGER

When couples come to the decision to divorce, the common denominator between them often is anger. To be able to carry out a major decision, one has to be or feel justified. Hence, it is very common for the individual who is perpetrating the divorce to create an anger story against the other spouse, justifying the decision to divorce. That leads then to a counter anger story by the spouse being divorced. One anger story will clash with the other's anger story. If unresolved, divorce is likely to follow the increasingly intense anger stories they create.

In counseling, it is important to help separate out the true aspects of the anger story from the false aspects of the story. It is also important to separate out the true need for protection from false perceptions, where protection very well may not be needed.

In separating out the stories, it is important that both individuals come to realize that their anger is not their children's anger. Their story is not the children's story. They each have their own anger and their own story designed to give credence to their desire to divorce. The children have their story too.

The essence of counseling then becomes one of story-telling nightmares. First of all, the therapist must separate out the truth from the false aspects of each story. It also requires the therapist to separate out the anger and the story of the adults regarding the children and each of the spouses.

Once the stories are separated and understood, the family can begin to function in a more healthy and constructive manner for the benefit of each. Only then can the family members move on and build a positive life story in the context of a healthy relationship.

Functional living now can be achieved as compared to living in a dysfunctional and anger-based remnant of a family.

MY COMMENT: Remember, your story may not be the true story. Under stressful times only true stories facilitate healing. Untrue stories are created for a purpose and have a harmful impact.

47.
I DATED MY WIFE, BUT MARRIED MY JOB

Today, I met with two men separately about three hours apart, both of whom fit this particular statement. They both were highly devoted to their employment, their occupation, and their future occupational career. While they were married and appreciated their wives and their families, they both came to realize and admitted that their priorities were out of whack. Their jobs became number one and the focus of their energies and attention, while the wife and the family came second, third, and even fourth in their range of priorities. Sometimes a friend even become more important than one's family or spouse.

This is unfortunate and deadly. If it's allowed to continue, disaster is the most likely outcome, including divorce and severance from the family. Both men realized that their lives needed to be fixed, brought under control, and better managed. Interestingly, both men talked of their lifestyle, but never broke down and cried as I expected. Regret was not an obvious emotion.

Therapy is now in order with the sequence of sessions focusing on life priorities, boundaries in living, the clarification of values, and the relevance of family. This includes a wife, children, and even the extended family. Therapy also needs to focused on developing the ability to say "No" or "stop."

While it seems like a paradox, when one puts the marriage and family in proper perspective, employment and careers fall in line and also tend to do well. Unfortunately, it doesn't work the other way around.

MY COMMENT: Live by priorities, not impulse of pleasure and interests.

48.
LEARNING TO EXPRESS GRATITUDE IN A MARRIAGE

During my counseling with a mid-age couple recently, I focused my attention on the degree to which they encouraged each other and showed gratitude and thanksgiving to each other and for each other, and for how each contributed to the richness of their mutual life.

To be sure, our world today is lacking in gratitude. We are a world of giving and taking, but little gratitude is expressed in the process. Somehow, we have missed the point. Also, we are not teaching our young people today to be thankful and grateful for what they have, what they receive, what they are given, and the opportunities provided them within their home, school, church, and general community.

In the process of the counseling sessions, I encouraged the couple to begin a gratitude journal in which they would record daily something for which they are grateful. They were to do this for an entire week. At the end of each week, they were to share with each other what they had written daily during the week. This exercise was designed to help them begin to think of gratitude and to begin the process of expressing it in written as well as verbal form.

Ultimately, my goal this exercise was to help them become more verbally expressive of gratitude and thankfulness for each other and for the things each of them contributed to the relationship each day.

MY COMMENT: If we take time to think, we will have time to express gratitude.

49.
DO STICKS AND STONES REALLY HURT OTHERS?

Today, I was talking with Jenny who unfolded the story of an 8-year marriage in which she was repeatedly abused to the point that she finally had enough and ended the relationship. We spoke of the reasons she didn't end the marriage before eight years and also how she was able to handle it.

In her responses to my questions during the therapy sessions, a childhood adage seemed appropriate and applied to her situation. In some ways it might sound like a putdown or a simplistic reply, but in her situation it was relevant and applicable, "Sticks and stones will break my bones, but names will never hurt me."

This adage was helpful because she was not beaten up physically, but was attacked through words, name calling, hurtful sarcasm, criticism, and painful words spoken to her by her husband. She thought she was strong and able to resist these attacks. While she did for a while, she soon began to weaken as the hurt piled up and eventually broke her.

I used this adage as a way to not minimize what happened to her, but to put it into perspective. Thankfully, she was not physically abused. In some ways, thankfully she was only abused through name calling and putdowns because that means of abuse can be processed and put into perspective. She eventually was able to move beyond it. It was important for her not to believe such attacks on her character. The attacks spoke more of her husband's character then hers.

We then engaged in conversation as to how she can minimize these words lingering in her memory and actually move forward in her life, in spite of the name calling to which she was subjected. The process was hard and arduous, but she stuck with it and came through as a whole person. Healing from pain is always slow when it is primarily a chronic emotional hurt. However, healing does require directly facing the areas of hurt and pain. It also requires the decision to take no more. Finally, it requires a change in lifestyle and behavior of the part of both or certainly the one who is the victim. No more is the byword.

MY COMMENT: Remember that the sticks and stones of life hurt and sting, but they do not break your spirit and determination.

50.
A FINANCIAL PLAN IS A NECESSARY TOOL IN A MARRIAGE

Early in therapy with a person, it becomes obvious that what is needed is a financial plan. Either there is uncontrolled spending, irresponsible financial management, the absence of a plan for saving, or the gross lack of adequate income.

I find in therapy what is shown in the various surveys conducted over the years about wills and trusts. 40% of the population has a will when 100% of the population actually need to have a will in place before they die. Having a trust is not necessary for many people, but, at times and in certain situations it is a very appropriate and a proper financial instrument.

As I become aware of the need for financial management, I encourage patients to create their own will. The necessary form is available on the internet and available in local stationary stores. It is easy to create your own will. It is necessary and appropriate particularly if you have income, if you have savings, and if you have children.

A referral to an attorney is often necessary and most appropriate and needs to be considered.

As a therapist, I have the responsibility that goes beyond the therapy issues of a session and the original purpose for coming to therapy. I also have a responsibility to help my patients be responsible for their own financial resources and assets and for protecting and caring for their family. Having a will and/or a trust is certainly one important component to do this.

MY COMMENT: Be sure you have a will and/or trust if you have children, property, a substantial savings account, and/or an estate of wealth.

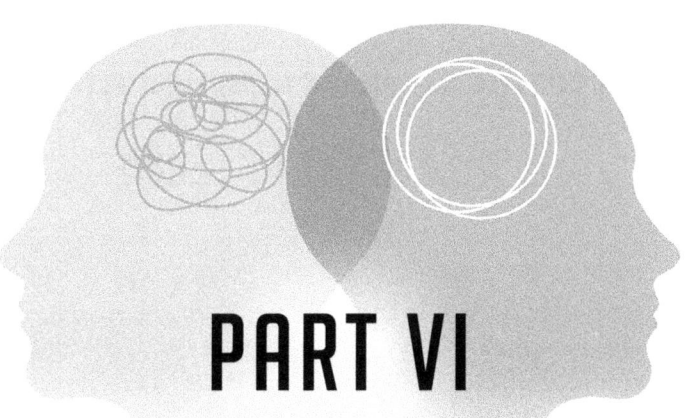

PART VI

CAN THERAPY HELP ME IMPROVE MY FAMILY LIFE AND PARENTING?

51.
EFFECTIVE FAMILY COMMUNICATION IS NECESSARY TO LEARN

I find this topic being a frequent issue to discuss with a wide variety of patients, young, middle-aged, and old age. Some people are born into a family of communicators. They talk. They listen. They interact. They consider opinions and ideas of each other. They learn from each other. They are an engaged family.

However, unfortunately, many people are born into a family of non-communicators. Feelings, events, and ideas are not expressed or spoken about. In fact, they are discouraged and ignored. Such families tend to be dull and ineffective in almost all areas of life. Family members are more likely to go elsewhere to experience engagement and interpersonal interchange. Many are resigned to a life of loneliness and interpersonal distancing.

Children raised in these two types of families are obviously very different. Kids raised in a communicating family communicate freely. They learn communication skills. Kids raised in a non-communicating family do not relate to the broader family, but live a life of withdrawal and isolation. They go elsewhere to find someone with whom to interact. Such family life is a recipe for disaster.

What is the objective that I try to achieve, in working with marriages and individuals, where communication is a problem?

Here's the formula: First, one must learn to express themself appropriately to the situation they are in at the time. Situational cues are vital to observe and respond to at the time.

Secondly, one must learn to speak favorably and positively when needed. Yes, there are times to speak up and encourage a conversation and encourage a particular behavior pattern.

Thirdly, one must learn to be able to speak words of correction and words of caution when appropriate. There are also times to speak up and discourage a particular behavior pattern and an activity that is taking place.

For effective communication, one must be ready to speak the words necessary and appropriate for the occasion. One must have the skill, experience, and the encouragement to speak up and be the voice of reason, the voice of reality, and, the voice of correction, the voice of encouragement, when needed. The idea of being ready to speak means that you do what is necessary to acquire the skill to speak, then have the insight for what needs to be said at any given time.

Of all the skills kids need to learn, assertive communication is most likely the most important.. Without such skill, a child is vulnerable to the powers and will of others all his life. I see such neglect as a form of passive child abuse by the parents. It is a deliberate act of neglect to leave a child subject to the powers of others and under the control of others.

The best way to learn to communicate is by using behavioral rehearsal. That is to practice talking and interacting starting with simple comments and statements and then going on to more complex verbal statements. Start with people you know such as family and friends, and then go on to strangers.

Families need to make good use of mealtimes to communicate, such as sharing the events of the day, planning activities, discussing the news of the day, and the needs and problems of the neighborhood and community.

MY COMMENT: Stop blaming your past, learn to speak up and do it daily.

52.
DYSFUNCTIONAL FAMILIES CREATE DYSFUNCTIONAL FAMILIES

One of the great pains I experience as a therapist is to counsel a dysfunctional and fractured family. Dysfunctional families lack bonding, togetherness, joy, cooperation, support, and many other qualities that bring people together, bonding them around a common purpose and value. It is usually generational.

As I work with a patient from such a background, there is always the question, "Can it be fixed? What can be done about it? Can I help fractured family members live with and beyond a fractured legacy? For any such patient, it is their role to live above it and live better than any of their family members. In other words, it is vitally important for a family member not to perpetuate historical pattern of dysfunctional living. It is my role to teach functional communication, decision making, and relationships.

This was the case for Jane when she came to therapy shortly after a family get-together over Christmas. The dysfunctional relationships prevailed and were overwhelming for her. She finally saw the impossibility of trying to live within the context of this "crazy" family life, if she was going to survive and create her own family to live functionally.

As we talked, I helped her think through her past and future role within the context of the dysfunctional family. We also viewed the option of disassociating from the family except for very rare and important events. We looked at the unreasonableness of even thinking she could play a constructive role and rehabilitate the dysfunctional family.

As we viewed these options, it became very obvious to her that her own survival and her own family life depended on her disassociating from her primary family. Yet she had to think through how to maintain the option of being part of the family activities if it were something essential, such as a funeral, a wedding, or a serious medical condition of one of the family members. Other than those types of situations, she decided to remain independent, separate, and avoid all contact with the primary family. Instead, she decided to spend much time with several friends.

I saw Jane about six to eight months later and found out that she had not only honored the agreement, but that it worked. She was feeling less depressed, less stressed, and more empowered as a wife and mother in the context of her own family.

The reality is to know that there are things that cannot be fixed, whether they be objects, people, or relationships. Another reality she had to face is that she was not in a position to fix the primary family, even if it could be fixed. It would need to be fixed by a third party, perhaps a professional. Unfortunately, such dysfunctional families do not come to therapy for such help even if they know they are dysfunctional.

It is also important to recognize what you can do and what you cannot do. What is possible and what is not possible through your efforts and involvement, needs to be clearly recognized.

It is vitally important to know that you cannot repeat the dysfunctional lifestyle of your childhood. Healing and living beyond the dysfunction and living functionally, happily, joyfully, successfully, and productively is the goal and essential objective for a person. A healthy life rather than being absorbed in a history of dysfunctional living is imperative living.

MY COMMENT: If it is dysfunctional, avoid it, change it, or live above it.

53.
GAMING VS. SOCIAL MEDIA IN THE HOME

Mr. and Mrs. Novato were no different in their concern for their kids than any parent I see in my clinical practice regarding their junior high and high school student, they asked me, "How much video, gaming, and social media is appropriate and healthy?"

This question always gives me opportunity to review again the research that came out of Australia several years ago indicating that teenagers who excessively engage in video gaming increase in their grades and in their academic scores from year to year. However, students who engage in a high degree of daily social media actually decrease in their grades and academic scores over the years of high school.

Based on this research, I tell parents to encourage limited gaming and discourage social media, as much as possible. Limiting gaming to three hours daily is very important and appropriate. Social media needs to be limited even more so. It is interesting to note that China has a limit of one and a half hours daily for such video and cell phone usage by their youth.

Parents need to know and be in control as to what their kids are doing so they can guide them in appropriate use of computer time, both in and out of the home. Along this line, I also encourage parents to be well informed about the content of any and all games being used and any and all topics being viewed and engaged in on social media. When such topics and media are sexual, hostile, violent, abusive, or angry, for example, the parent needs to step in and stop all exposure to such content. This is a good time to discuss appropriate computer use with them.

This requires a timely and detailed discussion as to why such content is inappropriate and must stop. Furthermore, parents must model in their own life and viewing appropriate use of the computer and all types of video viewing.

One last point, when a parent discovers inappropriate content on their child's cell phone or computer, it is vital that the parent contact the parents of their friends and other kids involved in the computer game or media interchange. Let all parents know what you found and what you did about it. Encourage them to do likewise.

MY COMMENT: Control the time kids have on their computers and how they use their time gaming and engaging in social media interchange.

54.
BULLY BEHAVIOR MUST BE ADDRESSED

In talking with a father today regarding his children, it was discovered that his boys have been the object of bully behavior at school for several years. He did not know this as his boys did not tell him of their being so threatened and mistreated. Once he learned of their experiences, things changed.

Here's what he told his boys, and I've heard this from other parents as well, "If anybody bullies you again, I want you to take them down and beat them up so they'll never do that to you or anybody else again." The dad followed this statement, which makes good sense, with this comment: "Know this, I will back you up at school and anywhere. You are not to be bullied and don't let anybody do it to you." I added to our discussion, "Don't let anyone take your peace away."

In my professional experience, I have found that school authorities do little to defend a child from being bullied or to stop bullying behavior once it starts. Kids are on their own by and large. They have to rely on themselves or their parents. That is why I always involve parents in this issue when their child is being bullied. The parents have to step forward and take charge and stop this kind of behavior. Parents cannot rely on the school as the school administration does little. Unfortunately, school administrators do not know what to do in such situations.

Essentially, parents are to teach self-protective, self- defensive, assertive behavior, and avoidance behavior in such situations in the first place.

Here's the real issue. A child needs to learn how to stand up for himself, but he also has to know that he has back-up that's reliable, dependable, available, and forceful. That is the primary role of the father in the life of a kid. So, dads, if your kid is being bullied, take charge. Stop it. Don't wait for the school principal to step in. Don't rely on the school. Teach your child how to negotiate with bullies and such peers. It is a lifetime issue for many, unfortunately.

In talking with another parent recently on this same subject, here's another point that is worthy of consideration. This parent said, "I told my kid that if he gets beat up that's not the worst thing that ever happens. If you play football you're going to get beat up. If you wrestle, you're going to get beat up. If you play soccer, you're likely to get beat up, as these are contact sports. You'll heal, you'll get better, and you'll be better for it. You'll learn how to take and you'll learn how to suffer, but you will also learn how to get up and get going again." That's resilience.

So, for a parent, you need not protect your child totally, and you need to back-up your child totally. However, you do need to teach assertive behavior and communication skills. Kids need to be proactive for their own good.

> **MY COMMENT:** No more bully behavior, defend yourself, but have a back-up.

55.
THE COST OF CRITICISM IS SET BY THE CHILD IN THE HOME

Recently, I met with a young couple regarding the conflict they are experiencing in raising their children. The mother tended to be very complimentary, supportive, and unconditionally encouraging towards the children. The father tended to be much more critical and prone to frequently use physical punishment as well as other forms of punishment.

In the course of my discussion with them, I reminded them of some recent research in the area of interpersonal criticism, and, in particular, how it applies to parenting. I recounted for them the study in which the researchers found that children who are physically punished or severely criticized require at least four statements of praise and affirmation for each criticism or punishment. Further, some children require not four praises but perhaps six or ten, or perhaps even twelve for each criticism and/or physical punishment they receive at home. Every child has their own "price tag" for being criticized or put down by a parent, or anyone else.

Unfortunately, in this couple as well as in others, the parent who was most prone to criticize or physically punish a child also found it difficult to praise or affirm their child for anything. They seemed to be stuck on the negative approaches to child discipline and find it almost impossible to speak words of kindness, gentleness, affirmation, and encouragement and support.

For this couple, the significant difference between them and their style of discipline needed to be addressed. While it is easy to support one and not support the other, it is important in therapy to help them come together and blend together their strategies of child discipline. In other words, how to get one to be more complimentary and become more temperate or moderate in the execution of punishment or discipline is the critical issue for many parents? How do you support one of the couples in being positive and complimentary while not trying to show favoritism in the course of therapy?

Yes, as a therapist, I must try to keep the compliments flowing. Keep the compliments flowing from both parents. If punishment is to be used as a disciplinary measure, see that it is done consistently, fairly, and is agreeable to both parents.

With the use of punishment, a parent needs to know how to redeem the child and their relationship with the child. Somehow good needs to come from any and all punishment.

MY COMMENT: In the long run, criticisms are costly; so, prefer compliments.

56.
COMPUTERS IN THE HOME CAN BE DISASTEROUS

Mr. and Mrs. Geneva raised the question in the family therapy session as to the use of Tik Tok by their two kids. They viewed it as another opportunity for the kids to be creative, build social relationships, but also, unfortunately, be exposed to serious mischievous activities.

Tik Tok and other social media is an opportunity for kids, in a very brief period of time, to create a scenario through which to interact with other students their age. Unfortunately, many students use this as an opportunity to create violence, aggression, and acts of destruction. For example, a recent Tik Tok production appears to have suggested or implied that students should engage in acts of destruction and violence on their school property including the breakage of bathroom porcelain and writing violent messages on the walls. Many students picked up the idea and pursued it accordingly. If such behavior is carried out it is generally done without the parent's knowledge. A major TV station picked up this style of influence of kids and aired it to alert parents of this influence on their children.

As I told this couple, parents need to be very much aware of what their kids are doing on their computers. Parents need to make sure that computer time is public and in an open space in the home. In other words, the computer is to be maintained in a place where it can be seen and monitored by the parents. The same goes for cell phone usage. Parents need to have open access to the cell phones of their kids. Phones logs need to be reviewed regularly.

For parents, it must be underscored that we are not living in the same world as they did as children. We are in a new age of technology with its advantages as well as its host of potential destruction and problematic behavior.

MY COMMENT: Computer use needs to be an open family matter.

57.
VIDEO GAMING CAN BE GOOD, BUT MUST BE CONTROLLED

When I met with Elvira regarding her teenage son. She expressed concern about him because he spends hours and hours playing games on his videos. True, she needs to be concerned. Hours on gaming keeps a child from having social relationships which are very important during the developmental years. It also keeps kids from engaging in creative activities and learning many of the self-help skills. Hence, these kids neglect learning advanced independent living skills.

However, based on an extensive study in Australia, gaming overall is a good thing, but it must be used in moderation. Moderation means about 2 to 3 hours a day, not 5, 8, or 10. Gaming teaches a child how to strategize, problem-solve, think ahead, engage in forethought, and work on problems and their solutions.

Research shows that children who game reflect an increase in test scores and overall academic progress (see above). Gaming helps the brain develop in the forebrain area which is associated with problem-solving, forethought, and strategizing skills. Grades tend to go up accordingly.

However, for the teenagers who spend hours and hours on social media, the opposite tends to occur. Grades and academic learning tend to go down. Social skills are still learned best in real life social relationships.

This is an area of parenting that needs to improve and be a focus of parents' attention and monitoring.

MY COMMENT: Parental involvement in their child's video activity is still an essential aspect of active parenting.

58.
THE ADOPTED CHILD IS AT RISK BUT THE RISK MUST BE MANAGED

Jonathan came for therapy soon after he learned at age 10 that he was adopted. He was quite emotional about this new discovery. He did not specify what led the adoptive parents to tell him of his adoption, but nonetheless they laid that on him fairly bluntly. They did so in a relatively cold and objective manner. This was very disturbing to him. Soon after that, he asked if he could go to a counselor and talk about it. His parents agreed. I was the counselor the parents selected due to some mutual contacts.

First of all, I am of the old school. I do not recommend telling children that they were adopted. If you feel you must tell them, wait until they are older, perhaps 21 or older. Young children do not have a context in which to understand adoption so they put their own spin on it, often to their own detriment. Many kids suffer great harm by learning too young in their life about their adoption.

This is what I told Jonathan. We talked about it and he could just not understand why his parents would tell him and why they told him in the way that they did. He agreed, life was going relatively well until he was "informed" of his adoptive status. This threw him for a loop. What did it mean? Was he a rejected child? Was he an abandoned child? Why would his parents not want him? What were his parents like? How did he get to be raised by these particular adoptive parents? Why did they adopt him and not somebody else? Why did they adopt and not have their own child? All these questions and more were discussed in a timely manner over several sessions.

These are the typical questions that any kid asks when they learn they have been adopted. I think Jonathan, as well as all children, should be spared of such trauma. Let life be lived out. If the adoption issue needs to be faced, do it when the child is older and has an adult perspective on life and understands the variety of ways in which children come into life, come into family life, and have purpose.

In a similar vein, I am also of the old school that says, if a child knows that he is adopted, he should not be encouraged to seek out or have connections with his natural parents who, by the way, are often very dysfunctional themselves. The whole issue of adoption is potentially traumatizing. I do not encourage that trauma to be activated during the child's younger years. But if the natural parent(s) need to be disclosed or discovered, it should be done when the child is well within his adult years. It should be done when he has full perspective on life, a well-established and stable lifestyle, an understanding of birth and adoption, and has well established mature behavior patterns himself.

Finally, if a child at some early age has to deal with the knowledge of his adoption, by all means the parents need to underscore the idea of the adoptive family being the child's "forever family." Families need to make a big thing out of being a "forever family." Celebrate it.

An adopted child also needs to learn of the happiness of the parents for the child's role and contribution to family life. What is the unique role the adoptive child plays in the life of the family? Ever family is different, but discussion on these matters can be wholesome.

MY COMMENT: Adoptive families need to be "forever families."

59.
QUESTIONS PARENTS NEED TO PONDER

Whenever I see parents in the office regarding their children, I look for opportunity to introduce several themes that I think are very important in the parenting process. Parents need to ponder several issues, one of which is how to turn their kid into a productive, successful, achieving, and happy person.

Here are several important issues for parents to ponder:

1. Does my child live a life of fun?

2. Does my child live a life of creativity?

3. Does my child live a life of kindness?

4. Does my child live a life of consideration for others?

5. Does my child live a life of intellectual curiosity?

6. Does my child live a life of values, ethics, and morals.

7. Does my child live a life of faith and God-honoring behavior?

Often parents in the mundane of everyday work, child-rearing, and family life forget that there is a higher value for children. Parents need to stimulate this type of thinking in no uncertain terms. It's an important aspect of parenting.

I am amazed at the number of parents who do not give thought to these kinds of issues in their day-to-day parenting in the home. They agree that these are very important values and behavior patterns to instill in their children, but they just don't do it. It is not until a therapist comes along and points out the importance of these kinds of behaviors and shows them how they can be instilled and encouraged in the course of day-to-day family living.

MY COMMENT: Use the dinner table to discuss issues and raise questions for the kids to ponder, stretch their imaginations, and resolve.

60.
DISABLED KIDS IN THE HOME REQUIRES FORETHOUGHT AND PLANNING

Periodically, I meet with a parent who has a child that is disabled in some manner and is in a state of dependency. Parents have all kinds of mixed emotions in such situations as they love their child, want to care for their child, but do not want to take away the child's chance of increased or full independence. It is important that the parent determines the level of independence possible and how they can work to achieve it. Hence, counseling becomes a very important component in this process, as many parents need the advice of a professional to guide them accomplish their goals.

It is my practice with good benefit to actually encourage parents, first of all, to determine the level of independence possible and develop a treatment or rehabilitation program to achieve that level of independence. Parents need to focus on the level of independence possible, not on the level of disability or dependency. The goal is always to reduce dependency.

Secondly, I recommend parents to consult their attorney and financial advisors to establish a Special Needs Trust for the child. Then they can begin to fund that trust so that in the parents' absence or inability to care for the child, there are funds that can be utilized to maintain the child at a given level of care. There are other forms of trusts as well, but a Special Needs Trust is a good place to start.

Thirdly, if a parent is financing a child's living expenses either in the home or in a semi- independent living situation and the child is old enough generate some income but is not doing their part, I then recommend that the funds put out by the parents for their child's monthly living expenses be carefully accounted for and taken out of the child's future inheritance. In other words, the child takes a portion of his inheritance now on a monthly basis. That can serve as a motivator for the child to generate some income as well as to appreciate that such funds for monthly living is really his or her responsibility as an adult. Further, such accounting is fair to the other children in the family so they are not deprived of their fair share of any inheritance.

Now there are special situations that requires very particular thought and consideration as well as advice from several different professionals. It is important that as a therapist I am able to point the family in the right direction and help them obtain the right kind of advice and care needed in their situation.

MY COMMENT: When seeking help in caring for a disabled child, be sure to consult those who know and have experience in the field of rehabilitation relevant to your child's problems, inabilities, and needs.

61.
PARENTING STYLES AND THE USE OF PUNISHMENT

I spoke with Joyce and Ed the other day regarding their parenting approach and parenting style. I got the feeling that there was a little bit too much emphasis on physical punishment. I commented about it with them and engaged them in a lengthy discussion on the issue. After some discussion, I did recommend that they begin to a more favorably utilization of "time out" rather than physical punishment.

The research is very interesting and very clear. Parents who use physical punishment with their children tend to have children who become more aggressive than children who were not raised on the use of physical punishment as a discipline strategy. For the parents who use "time out," there's an absence of depression, an absence of anxiety, and an absence of mental health issues in their children. They also tended to realign their behavior more appropriately after the use of "time out" was initiated as a primary disciplinary procedure.

"Time out" is placing the child in a low stimulation area such as a quiet room or in a secluded area until the child calms down and is ready to rejoin the activity of the family or activity that was taking place at the time they were misbehaving. In other words, this could be a matter of minutes or longer, it's up to the child. However, "time out" is usually about 5 to10 minutes after the child calms down and is under control once again. The child also needs to be ready to rejoin family life and behave appropriately.

MY COMMENT: Time out is better than most other forms of punishment.

62.
COUPLES ARE EFFECTIVE WHEN BOTH LEARN TO CONVERSE FREELY

Today I met with a young gentleman, age 25, who had a personal issue that needed to be sorted out. We had been talking for about 40 minutes on the issue of his concern and it appeared to me that he was not particularly comfortable talking about himself and the issues of his life.

Because of this observation, I asked him if he came from a talking family. He said, "No." He said his brother, his sister, his mother, and father are essentially non-talkers. The father is a little bit more talkative than the others. We then explored that a little bit more. What he meant by that was the idea that while he may talk, he doesn't talk about personal things. He does not share his life. He does not share his concerns. He does not share his worries or hurts. He does not share his problems.

We then looked at the relationship in which he is involved. He stated his girlfriend is not particularly a talker either. Herein lies potential difficulty. If he's not a talker and she's not a talker, how in the world are they going to resolve issues and deal with issues through debate, discussion, and controversy? How are they going to make decisions in life relative to their own personal preferences?

Basically, I said this, "Be careful that you don't marry somebody who is a non-talker and likewise don't marry somebody who's an excessive talker because either way it's going to be a difficult relationship." He needs to marry somebody who is a moderate talker, but will help him talk and be encourage him to share his life, thoughts, and feelings. He stated that his current girlfriend is of that nature and that he's now beginning to talk a little bit more than he ever has in the past. I praised him and urged more of it. Relationships thrive on the act of talking and sharing.

That leads me to say this, it's important that you become a conversant individual. You should learn that at home as a child, but if you don't, you have to learn it as an adult. You have no excuse not to become a conversant talking person. There are enough ways to learn it, there are enough people in your life to learn it from, and there is no excuse to go on in life being a quiet and withheld person who does not share thoughts and feelings as appropriate.

To help yourself become more of a talking person, read on the topic, listen to others, watch others talk, ask others how they learned to talk, and learn from movies and TV interviews.

MY COMMENT: Relationships thrive on talking. Be a talker.

63.
COMMUNICATION BASED ON ONE-LINERS CAN BE POWERFUL

Today, I spoke with Julie whose husband is on his death bed. We talked about the years of their marriage and family life. We identified many areas of positive strengths and what identified him throughout the life of the family and to her personally. It came down to one-liners – "He was a man of one-liners."

One-liners are often used to rear children. He used them well in his relationship to his family. While he didn't have much to say regarding the family's living arrangement and behavior patterns, he often drew the line by stating a one-liner. It was his words for the kids – "Don't go further." "Don't you dare." "Don't try it."

Actually, fathers are usually the ones that set the limit and set the pace in family life. Fathers are generally the ones to give kids models to live by. Fathers are the ones to draw a line and give kids the word that they've reached the end of the line, and they should go no further. They set the boundary. They determine the barrier.

Mothers and fathers must work well together for kids to thrive. Mothers usually handle the day-to-day life, see that all goes well, and manage homelife to be well-coordinated. Fathers usually step in when a line needs to be drawn, when the word of authority is needed, or when the limit has been reached. When the two are coordinated, a win–win situation emerges for all. Mothers need that kind of back-up. Kids need the strength that comes from the father when he draws the line, often by using a "one-liner."

In contrast, the absence of such a parental coordinated effort is what contributes to kids being problematic in our society, defiant within the home and school, and non-achievement oriented in their lifestyle.

MY COMMENT: Home life functions best for all family members when mom and dad define their roles and play them consistently.

64.
THE COST OF CRITICISM IN THE HOME

One day I met with a young couple regarding the conflict they were experiencing in raising their children. One parent tends to be very complimentary, supportive, and encouraging towards the children. The other parent tends to be much more critical and prone to use physical punishment and other fairly restrictive forms of punishments.

In the course of my discussion with them, I reminded them of some recent research in the area of interpersonal criticism and in particular how it applies to parenting. I recounted the study in which the researchers found that children who are physically punished or severely criticized require at least four statements of praise and affirmation for each criticism or each punishment to help them recover. Further, there are some children who require not four praises, but perhaps six, ten, or even twelve, for each criticism and/or physical punishment. Every child has their own "price tag" for being criticized and being able to forgive.

Unfortunately, in this couple as well as in others, the parent who is prone to criticize or physically punish a child finds it very difficult to praise or affirm the child at all for anything. They seem to be stuck in the negative approaches to child discipline and find it almost impossible to express words of kindness, gentleness, affirmation, and encouragement or support.

Secondly, in this couple the significant difference between them and their style of discipline needed to be addressed. While it is easy to support one and not support the other, it is important in therapy to help them come together and blend together their strategies of child discipline. In other words, how to get one to be more complimentary and how do you get one to become more temperate, moderate, or mild in the execution of punishment or discipline? How do you show support towards one as being positive and complimentary while not trying to show favoritism in the course of therapy or discourage the other one?

Yes, keep the compliments flowing. Get compliments to flow from both parents. If punishment is to be used as a disciplinary measure, see that it is done consistently, fairly, and is agreeable to both parents. Also, be sure to follow-up with adequate compliments for good behavior.

> **MY COMMENT:** In the long run, criticisms are costly; prefer to give many compliments.

65.
TOO MUCH PUNISHMENT IN THE HOME

Today, I saw a young boy, Carlos, age 8, who was brought to the appointment by his parents. He was defiant and there seemed to be no benefit from the discipline strategy they were using. The parents expressed their desperation for help when they called for an appointment.

As is typical, my first appointment was divided in half. Thirty minutes with the parents and thirty minutes with the child. This is essentially a fact-finding session, but I am on the hunt for the issues that are creating a strain on the family relationships and thus preventing this family from having a positive relationship together.

At the end of my first session after meeting with the parents and the child, it became very obvious to me what several of the issues were that needed to be addressed. Paramount however was the excessive use of punishment by the parents as their primary child management strategy. Far too little praise was being used.

To be sure, Carlos presented as a problem to the parents who were becoming increasingly exasperated in how to manage him. All efforts failed so they reverted to even more punishment as their "go to" strategy.

Therein lies one of the primary problems. The parents were trying to manage Carlos when they really should be managing Carlos' behavior. They are becoming increasingly angry at him and frustrated with him. They were treating him in a derogatory manner. All of this contributes to a very low self-esteem on the part of Carlos and fueled his defiance all the more. Unfortunately, the behavior did not change as the behaviors were not focused on for change.

In my second session, I met primarily with the parents. I spent 20 minutes with the child and 40 minutes with the parents. I looked for the first opportunity from my meeting with the parents to focus their attention on the negative strategy being used for child management. They were relying upon punishment for his inappropriateness. There was much of it, to be sure. I said to the parents, "Punishment tells the child what not to do, but never tells the child what to do." In the remainder of that particular session and the next session or two, my theme was, "Less punishment and more use of rewards and reinforcement for behavior that is appropriate."

As this change in strategy was used in the home, Carlos began to change. He began the process of engaging in more appropriate behavior allowing the parents to be even more reinforcing and rewarding to him for the improved behavior.

MY COMMENT: Parents need to focus on what punishment tells a child. Generally, punishment tells a child what not to do, but not what to do. Help the child do more good behavior and then reward the child for the appropriate behavior.

66.
MOTHER ARE THE EFFECTIVE "LESSON-GIVERS" IN THE HOME

It is all too common to meet with mothers when they bring their child for therapy. Today was no exception. The mother, Angela, came with your young 9-year-old son as he was becoming increasingly defiant in the home and also at school with the teacher. She was afraid, as I was, of this defiance increasing and becoming a major problem for the boy as well as for the family. She was right, it was time to bring in a professional family therapist to help her and her family deal with the issue and help the boy resolve some of the underlying anger that promoted the defiance.

In the course of my three or four sessions I had with the mother and the boy, I spent half of the hour with the mother and half of the hour with the boy. I drew upon an old adage that says, "Great lessons in life are often learned at the knees of the mother." The mother needed time to digest the meaning of that statement.

She had never heard this adage, so I began to unfold the meaning of it and apply it to her and her situation with her son. I spoke of the importance of the mother assuming the role of the "lesson-giver" in the home and with her children. We spent time together figuring out what great lessons she could teach her child and needed to teach her child. We spoke of ways for her to teach and implement lessons such as at bedtime chats, car time conversations, mealtime family interactions, and the time she wished him well and would say good-bye to the child as he was sent off to school each morning. Interestingly, as parents become more of a positive teacher in the home, they become better parents overall.

Over the course of three months, it became obvious that she was in fact teaching valuable lessons and the boy was responding. While in no way do we have a perfect child or a great outcome in family therapy. We did, however, see an improvement, and we did have cause to rejoice together in that improvement.

Unfortunately, the family moved and I was no longer able to continue counseling them but she was encouraged to continue the program of teaching great lessons to her children regularly in the home "at her knee."

MY COMMENT: Some kids just need to connect with the mother. There are many ways to do this. The knee is one of them.

67.
THE ROLE OF A GRANDPARENT IN THE PERSONAL DEVELOPMENT OF THEIR GRANDCHILDREN

Today I met with a set of grandparents of eight grandchildren, half of whom lived in the same geographic area while the other half lived considerably far away. They spoke of the commitment they had to doing something special with them together and with each grandchild separately as much as possible.

The grandchildren that were living at a distance were engaged by means of zoom as often as possible. They learned to Zoom so they could connect with the kids, quite a task for any grandparent. They did this for the past two years while the children were spending more time at home, as they were not attending regular school. This gave the grandparents an opportunity to build a bond, build stories, and build memories with their distant grandchildren that otherwise would not have been possible.

For the grandchildren in the area where they lived, they had a practice of grandpa taking the two boys out for breakfast or lunch while grandma took the two girls. This was a coordinated effort, and it worked well for them.

They spoke of the hour and a half they spent with their grandchildren on each of these occasions and the various conversations that ensued. They learned to relate to younger children and their grandchildren learned to relate to them as older adults. Certainly, it was a win-win situation. The bond between them grew stronger over time.

The grandparents also spoke of the lessons they have learned and things that they learned about their grandchildren that otherwise they may never have known. It was an event they always looked forward to on a monthly basis.

Before speaking about the issues for which they came for counseling, we did spend time reflecting on things that could be done with the grandchildren to enhance their times together. It would make it more meaningful for them as well as for the grandchildren. The options

ALLAN G. HEDBERG, Ph.D.

are innumerable. The list we drafted was quite lengthy and certainly welcomed by them. They welcomed new ideas and suggestions from my experience in doing something similar with my grandchildren and from my experience in counseling many grandparents over the years. Of particular note of interest for them was the idea of an annual trip for the grandkids together. This builds a bond like no other event.

MY COMMENT: Never discount the value and contributions of grandparents.

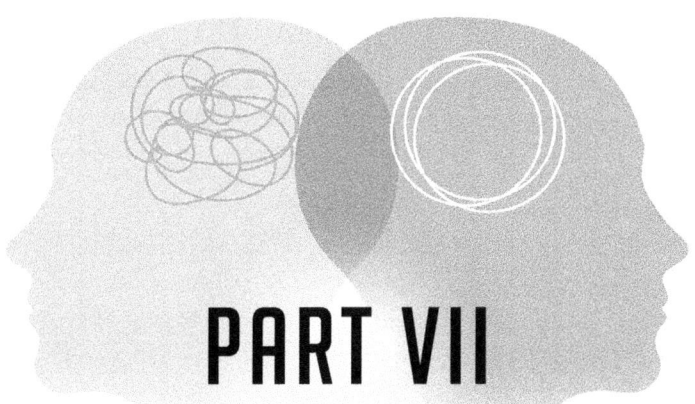

PART VII

CAN THERAPY HELP ME BETTER RESPOND TO SIGNIFICANT LIFE-CHANGING EVENTS?

68.
TIME FOR REFLECTION IS VALUABLE TIME

During the course of therapy, people experience major events in their life – marriage, births of children, deaths of family members, graduations, and other forms of accomplishment. As a therapist, I try to help people celebrate and commemorate times of accomplishment, achievement, and recognition. I also try to help them properly process the unpleasant experiences which promote sorrow and grief.

When I come to be aware of such situations in the course of my therapy, I generally engage patients in ways in which they can honor the event and the people involved through various forms of memorials, celebrations, and recognitions. For example, I often recommend the planting of a tree. I also recommend giving of funds to a charity in honor of someone whose life can continue to live through the financial support to a particular charity. I may also suggest the establishment of a memorial to which people can give in honor of the individual and his or her memory. There are multiple ways that people can celebrate and memorialize times, situations, and events in their life that give meaning, purpose, and value for those involved and for the general community.

I am amazed at the number of people I see in therapy who do not have a support system in place to celebrate their important events with them. That seems to prevail with the isolation and social withdrawal from people when one is depressed.

It should be noted that charities flourish on the gifts that come their way at times of such recognition. Churches do the same. There is value in making such donations and establishing such memorials. There is value for the patient in doing so. There is value for me as their therapist in recommending it and being a part of that decision, as well as value for those that benefit from the gift or contribution made in honor of someone.

Our world needs more giving. Our world needs more recognition given to loved ones and to those who have contributed to the welfare of others and to the betterment of one's community and society. This is one way and one time to do it. I particularly appreciate the value for the patient.

It gives meaning, a feeling of importance, and a feeling of improving the life of others. It's always a win-win situation.

The processing of painful experiences is of particular importance to address and not overlook or downplay. A therapist needs to be prepared to mourn with those who mourn.

MY COMMENT: Be sure to honor the life and achievements of those who have enriched your life.

69.
A CRIMINAL EVENT CAN FACILITATE A CHANGE IN BEHAVIOR PATTERNS

In today's session with John, he indicated that the Court had just confirmed his charge of a felony related to a sexual offense with children. That means, his opportunities for employment have been significantly restricted, if not impossible. In some ways, the Court creates more problems on top of the problem an individual is experiencing and for which he needs therapy. This is understandable, but still was a dilemma for John.

In talking with John today regarding the charge and the actions in which he was involved, it led me to the conclusion that his primary option for future work is self-employment rather than working for an employer where he would have to disclose the sexual offense and then be denied employment.

For John, self-employment was an interesting and unique option, but very difficult. He comes from a family with a history of "horse trading" and buying and selling off of the internet. So, we talked about ways in which this could be enhanced and maximized to the point that he could generate an income enough to live on. While there are many pitfalls in this kind of pursuit, it does represent an opportunity that he could develop immediately and not have to disclose to anybody his charge of a sexual offense.

Therapy is often a place of creativity. Every patient presents a creative problem that demands a creative answer. I hope this creative answer will serve well for John as he moves forward and tries to make life a satisfying experience as well as a way to generate self-support.

Come what may, he still has to deal with the charges filed against him, but as least he can earn money to live on in the meantime, which may be a year before it is resolved with the courts. Therapy can be the source of light along his path in rebuilding his life for a new future.

MY COMMENT: Even when circumstances are piling up against you, there are still avenues to pursue to keep your life going forward.

70.
RECOGNITION OF AN ACCOMPLISHMENT CAN ENHANCE A RELATIONSHIP

Periodically during the course of therapy, patients acquire a new car, a new truck, or some other major object; the pride of their life at the time. They worked hard for it, they have paid for it, and they cherished the moment when they were able to purchase their prized possession.

When a patient comes for therapy sessions having just acquired a prize possession, the patient wants to be celebrated for his ability to purchase that particular item, such as a car, truck, or home. They are excited and happy, and want you to be also.

That special attention gives a patient a sense of importance, acceptance, and a sense of value. It should not be overlooked. Therapists should not only acknowledge a special event like that but also capitalize on it. Patients like to be celebrated, honored, praised, and valued for what they are able to accomplish by hard work. They look to you for this adoration. Remember, a patient with a weak support system may not have received much praise from others. Hence, the attention you give to the occasion may mean a lot at the time.

A therapist would be wise to relate and tie together the purchase or the achievement, and then relate it to some element that has been a point of consideration during the therapy sessions. In other words, what is the nexus between the achievement and the purpose of therapy? What is the relationship between a valued purchase and the therapeutic issues that are under consideration? It's a teaching moment. It is an opportunity for growth, an opportunity for enhancement, and an opportunity for increased appreciation. A therapist should not miss that teaching opportunity.

A therapist would be wise to relate and tie together the purchase and the achievement, and relate it to some element that has been a point of consideration during the therapy sessions. In other words, what is the nexus? What is the relationship between a valued purchase and the therapeutic issues that are under consideration? It's a teaching moment, it's an opportunity for growth, an opportunity for enhancement, and it's an opportunity for increased appreciation. A therapist should not miss that teaching opportunity.

MY COMMENT: Look for every opportunity to celebrate with patients their personal achievements and relate them to other issues in their life being dealt with in therapy.

71.
THERAPY CAN HELP A PERSON COME TO TERMS WITH A TRAGIC LIFE EVENT

Vehicular manslaughter is a serious charge. Like many major accusations and charges against a person, it changes a person's life forever. This is true whether or not the accusation is correct or not.

Today, I met with Ernest who was referred to me by his attorney for treatment due to being recently charged with vehicular manslaughter following a major accident. In the first session, I asked him to tell me in his words what happened. He replied, "I killed someone. I was charged with vehicular manslaughter."

As he unfolded the story throughout the three therapy sessions, it became very apparent to me that Ernest did not "kill" someone. True, he was involved in an accident and it was his fault. He fell asleep while driving. True, a person died but it was an accidental collision and accidental death. He was not being irresponsible. He was not being dramatic. He was being expressly honest with me about the accident, so he thought.

As I reflected on this issue and Ernest's particular situation, it appeared to me that there is a difference between what Ernest did and the driver who deliberately and intentionally causes an accident because of his irresponsibility such as drunk driving and a person dies as a result. That is vehicular manslaughter. However, there are accidents which are purely coincidental and accidental. True, someone died but there was no intent or consideration whatsoever in bringing about that particular accidental event. That's a different matter. It is a serious matter, but a different accident- related criminal code applies.

To Ernest I said, "Yes, you were involved in an accident and a person died as a result of it, but it was not your intent or your deliberate action that caused the death. Therefore, you did not kill someone. Someone died in the accident in which you were involved."

Psychologically, it is very important for an individual to understand levels of responsibility and levels of seriousness when it comes to the results of their behavior. We need to accept corresponding levels of personal responsibility to the state, the victim, as well as to the family of the deceased or the victim, as in this case.

MY COMMENT: While we are to call a spade a spade, there are times when something looks like a spade, but is not a spade.

72.
CREATIVE WRITING CAN HELP BRING CHANGE TO A MORE POSITIVE LIFE STYLE

Today, I met with two young men about three hours apart from each other – one in the morning and one in the afternoon. Both of them were budding artists. One was writing music and the other was writing poetry. They did not know each other.

In speaking with them, we talked about a way in which ideas are generated and then converted into music or into a poem. We talked about ways in which they are encouraged by other people or discouraged in their writing process. We talked about the purpose of their writing and creativity. We talked about long-term potential.

While they didn't know each other and probably never will, they both share a degree of freshness and excitement when talking about their writing. Otherwise, there was a mode of depression that prevailed and that was really the purpose of their coming for the therapy week after week. It's been said, and to some degree this is true, people who are creative and artistic often have a prevailing degree of depression. The depression is usually not intense or debilitating, but mild and enough to interfere with the process of life for the individual. It is what we call low grade, chronic mild depression with which people can live and function – dysthymia. I would say that both of these young gentlemen were displaying dysthymia as a mood and both needed to learn how to live with it. They either have to learn to overcome dysthymia, live above it, or learn to live with it and not be debilitated by it. It must not be viewed as impairing, but rather like carrying a heavy load. A moderately heavy load.

Interestingly, over time in therapy as their writing progressed and improved over time, so did their dysthymia. They were beginning to feel like they could accomplish something, that they were successful, that they were noticed and made to feel important, and that they could accomplish something. That outcome in therapy overcomes dysthymia any time.

MY COMMENT: Use and advance your skills to combat unwanted emotions.

73.
CELEBRATION IS A VITAL PART OF A PERSON'S LIFE

As patients continue in their therapy program, events and things happen in their life. Certainly, there are many unpleasant and stressful events which occur which then need to be addressed, understood, and processed so the patient can move forward. Getting stuck in new stresses is always possible and needs to be addressed in a timely manner.

On the other hand, a number of events also occur in the life of a patient that cause them to feel very good and are worthy of being shared with you as their therapist. It is important to be alert to these kinds of events and celebrate them together when they occur.

Most recently several events came to my attention by several patients who volunteered information that was cause for celebration. Here are a few examples:

1. The announcement of a first pregnancy.

2. Paying off the mortgage of a house.

3. Increased assertiveness on the part of a patient's adult daughter in dealing with a very unpleasant situation in her life.

4. A son being accepted into a significant university of his choice.

5. Speaking up to a family member that has been the source of much pain and distress to the entire extended family.

6. Receiving an apology from a former friend after 2 years of a strained relationship.

7. The settlement of a legal suit that was long in coming.

8. A long awaited marriage after years of waiting for the right man to come into her life.

There are many such events that occur during the course of therapy. The important thing for the therapist is to become aware of them and spend a moment celebrating. It is important for the moment of celebration to be relevant to the situation for which they came for therapy in the first place. It is also very important that the therapist help them relate their situation to their celebration.

MY COMMENT: Celebrate the success and achievements of others as you would want to be celebrated if it was your success experience.

74.
THE DEATH OF A LOVED ONE CAN BRING NEW OPPORTUNITIES AND DEVELOPMENT

Today I discussed the meaning of "being dead yet speaketh" came to life. I met with an older gentleman whose sister had recently passed away. They had a close relationship, but it was a relief overall. While the relationship was not particularly strong and the sister did not play an intermediary role with the extended family, much came to life following her death.

Within three months he was contacted by the extended family living in the Midwest. They wanted to renew relationships with the extended family and he was first on the list. That has led to six or eight lengthy telephone calls renewing family history, and recalling past events that were meaningful to him as well as to the extended family. They both had much to learn from each other.

These calls and discussions opened up doors of information and opportunity to reconnect with the whole extended family. It was like a revival. New life within a family is exciting to see.

We both came to the conclusion that though his sister died she still speaks, but speaks through the extended family to him and he to them. She was a catalyst even though these discussions had not taken place during her lifetime.

This story is so true with a lot of people. Death is an opportunity to revive relationships, renew old acquaintances, to clarify points of confusion, to rebuild history, to explain history, and most of all to give a sense of continuity to one's life within the context of family.

Every therapist needs to be alert to the opportunities presented at the time of a death. It is a time of grieving, to be sure, but it's also an opportunity for new relationships and new perspectives. The revival of old relationships may now have meaning in a different way. Take advantage of the opportunity. Delve into the life of the family at the time of the death of a loved one of your patients. It is a very important endeavor for healing to be promoted. It is a very important opportunity for clarification and for meaning to come into the life of all extended family members.

MY COMMENT: Use every opportunity to create new stories and rebuild relationships.

75.
BE TRUE TO YOURSELF AND OTHERS

Today I was talking with Michael who stated that his grandmother was having her 89th birthday and he was being encouraged by his mother to send his grandmother a birthday card or gift. The problem however was that Michael did not like his grandmother. She has been unkind to him and, as a result, he has no particular feelings of goodness towards her. What should he do?

First of all, be true to yourself, I told him. If you want to be a person known for social grace and doing the right thing, then send a greeting to her. However, you also have to be realistic. If you don't feel particularly good towards her, it would not be sensitive or honest to send her a lavish gift or gushy card. A simple card instead might be more appropriate. The point that I was making was to do what is comfortable, do what is right for the situation, and do what you can honestly feel good about.

After much discussion, we decided that the most appropriate way to send a greeting to grandma was to text grandma a 4-word message related to happy birthday. We also agreed that he should not say things that he does not believe or does not feel, but just be true and be gracious.

I then went on to talk about how he needs to establish a pattern for himself for years ahead. No matter if he gets a card in return or a thank you note in return, do what is right for you and how you want to be known.

Generally speaking, it would probably be a good position to regularly send a greeting or a message of congratulations, when appropriate, but keep it very conservative. Keep it brief.

I ended our discussion by the issue of making sure that he does not try to sell a message to grandma or anyone else but to just deliver it. Send the message however, but don't try to elaborate or to create some kind of an image where you're trying to sell yourself or make yourself look good or say something that is not true. The important thing is, deliver the message of congratulations, but don't try to oversell the message or yourself.

MY ADVICE: Be true, be honest, be sincere, and be forgiving.

76.
THE STORMS OF LIFE CAN TRIGGER NEEDED CHANGE

Jane talked much today about changes that have taken place in her life over the past 35 years. Some were happy and welcome experiences, some were not. Nonetheless, we discussed each one and how it affected her and her family. We looked at the actual events and how they came about. These, she referred to them as, "the storms of life."

Several principles easily came forth from our three-session in which we discussed these events. Here they are:

- Any and all events can change your life if you allow it to change.

- Change can be for the good or bad of those involved.

- Be not afraid of life-changing events, but give them time to have their affect.

- Seek out the deeper meaning of life events; see the spiritual and the situational meaning of what took place.

- Ask, "Where is God in all this?"

- Keep going forward in life; always trying to learn a new lesson from each event.

- Life is not defined or determined by one event, neither are you.

- Review all events from the perspective of "a world view."

As we concluded our sessions on this topic, Jane felt great relief and gained a new appreciation for herself and her life experiences, good and bad.

MY COMMENT: Be not afraid to look under the surface of an event and learn from it.

77.
KEEP YOUR RELATIONSHIPS BALANCED

You are in charge of your life and the impact of events on you. You need not see yourself as helpless and vulnerable. You need not succumb to the forces of the events in your life. You can take charge and manage how you will be affected by any event or experience.

This idea was new to Jacob. He never thought of asserting himself and speaking up for himself. He was raised to just take life as it comes. He was not taught to seek out certain kinds of experiences or avoid certain experiences. Life was what it was, according to his very passive parents.

As our sessions continued and we spoke about this theme, I outlined several principles for living which I thought would be helpful to him in the long run. Here they are:

- If your feelings get hurt, step up and speak up; clear up any misunderstandings or misperceptions.

- You can still be happy even if all areas of your life are not happy.

- No matter what the circumstances, always show love an appreciation, especially to those close to you.

- Frequently check the "feeling-gauge" of your spouse.

- Feelings are not always the most accurate gauge of how one is experiencing life; it is better to check the actual behavioral patterns and life style, as well.

- Compare life style and life experiences over time; consider the trend of the changes for the good and the bad.

MY COMMENT: Relationships are to be evaluated over time for their trends and for any repairs needed.

ALLAN G. HEDBERG, Ph.D.

78.
UNEXPECTED PROBLEMS CAN
PROMOTE NEEDED CHANGE

Today, I had the occasion to talk to a middle-aged, well-experienced, junior high school teacher. He has taught many years.

Most unfortunately, he was accused of touching at least two girls which led to him being terminated from his employment with the school district and forced him into a legal battle which he eventually prevailed and was exonerated. However, his career was terminated and his credential revoked.

In the course of our discussion today, he reflected on what he has done since he was terminated from the school district and how he has developed a new career and a new pathway of life. Further, he has entered into a personal therapy program and has benefited significantly from it. He feels like he is a very different person than he was at the time that these events were claimed to have occurred. His therapy picked up at that point and change was soon forthcoming. The change did, however, require him to acknowledge what he did and how it affected the victim. He also had to come to terms with how it could have been prevented and what he could have done to reduce to hurt to the victim. We did consider how he will avoid and prevent such situations in the future.

MY COMMENT: While pain is unwanted, look for any good that can come from it.

79.
BE EFFECTIVE IN ALL SITUATIONS

As a therapist, I am committed to living a life consistent with positive mental health, effective social relationships, and a kindly personal manner. This is true whether I'm in the office with a patient, relating to my colleagues or family, or relating to the general public as I come and go throughout the community.

Today was no exception. I was in the gym preparing to do my exercises and had an interchange with the staff member checking me in. I know that he is a student but not in school at the present time. I know he plans to return to school next semester. Periodically, I encourage him to keep in mind the importance of his higher education and its benefit for the long run.

Today, I again approached the topic of his preparedness to return to school this semester. He said he was. I commended him for that and then I added a discussion point of saying "this is where you are supposed to be." Schooling is important and he's supposed to do it for his own sake as well as for the sake of his family. He seemed to resonate to my repeated phrase, "Be where you're supposed to be."

That is true for all of us. It is important that we pursue a path of understanding of where we're supposed to be at any given time. The benefits will follow.

As you know, it is easy to be somewhere else than where you need to be or are supposed to be. To get out of the pattern of life and not be where we're supposed to be is easy. It's so true for many of us. I repeat, "Be where you're supposed to be." Focus. Focus. Focus. The good things in life will follow. The misdeeds and trouble will go away.

MY COMMENT: Be where you are supposed to be. Focus. Focus. Focus.

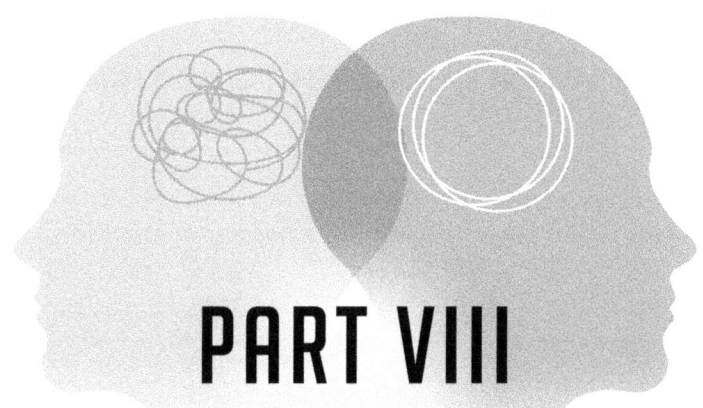

PART VIII

CAN THERAPY HELP ME MAKE BETTER BUSINESS DECISIONS?

80.
IS A BUSINESS PARTNERSHIP FOR ME?

Today, a young gentleman spent an hour with me regarding some highly personal areas of his life that had been a burden to him for years. In fact, the stress of these events and the stress from a few other problems where overwhelming. He was essentially disabled by these events and his attempt to justify them was no longer working. He felt despair and was disabled.

As he discussed and unfolded his story, he told of a partnership in which he became involved related to his business. It was marked with many problems and unresolvable stresses. The partner did not work as hard as he did. The partner did not volunteer to initiate activities, tasks, and business development, as he did, and so on. In other words, it became a disaster soon after the partnership was formed and after the business started up.

Not only did the business fail within the first year, but he became physically sick and nonfunctional. He developed a skin disorder and severe irritable bowel syndrome. It took him 6 months of psychotherapy with me and much medical treatment to heal to the point where he could work again.

It is well-known that partnerships are a high-risk undertaking. In his case, he concluded that a partnership is like "a ship that does not float." He decided to avoid the partnership idea.

His advice was to stay away from partnerships. If you can't do it yourself, don't do it at all was his advice. If you want to develop a business and undertake some kind of a project and you must have a partner, then don't do it, it's not worth it. That was his conclusion. Do it, however, if you can go it alone.

MY COMMENT: While the business of a partnership may be valid, the partners may not be.

81.
LEADERSHIP IS LEARN AND CONTRIBUTES TO INDEPENDENT LIVING

You can tell a leader when you see one. Nathaniel was no exception. He clearly demonstrated in his initial session that he was developing leadership skills and was well on his way to becoming a person of influence. He demonstrated assertive communication, problem-solving, decision-making, independent thinking skills, and self-confidence.

Unfortunately, Nathaniel was a victim of a bitter divorce. For years, he had to raise himself and his two siblings either due to the absence or passivity of his parents. They were too involved in their own anger and creating a divorce scenario for the marriage and the family.

I took the path of encouraging Nathaniel to recognize and appreciate the basic skills that he possesses, not only of leadership but of independent living. I encouraged him by saying that he will do well in life despite the inadequacies and trauma created by his parents. It is important for him to forgive his parents, overlook their dysfunction, and be grateful for the independent living skills and leadership skills he has developed. This is in spite of his parents' lack of parenting skills and commitment to him and his siblings.

Nathaniel and I spent six hours together over the course of his therapy. After the first session, we invited his parents to attend, but they refused. That told me even more that Nathaniel was indeed living a life uphill. Thankfully, he had the necessary determination to move upward on his own.

The lesson in life is the fact that we can develop positive behavior patterns, attitudes, and values in spite of the fact that our primary source of influence, our parents, are dysfunctional and destructive. It's a paradox, even dysfunctional, but it does require the learning of and utilization of many key independent living skills.

MY ADVICE: We can all achieve in spite of our parents' dysfunctional life style and their failure to teach successful living.

82.
HONEST AND SINCERE FARM LABORERS ARE NEEDED

Today, I spoke with a farmer in Central California. At the time, we had been over a year into the COVID pandemic. Workers were nowhere to be seen. No one wanted to work. They were all getting subsidies from the government, so they did not have to work. Why should they work?

I asked him if some of the migrants coming across the border illegally were beginning to filter up into our area in Central California to look for work. His response surprised me. He said, "I would rather take a young man coming across the border, preferably from El Salvador, than those that have been here for two, three, four, or more years." He added, "The longer they are here, the more they learn the handout system and take advantage of it."

Now that remark surprised me, so I inquired even more. He said this, "The ones that are coming now don't know the system, and they don't know how to con the system. They don't know the legal system and how to take advantage of it. They don't know the workers' compensation system to take advantage of it. They don't know how to take advantage of the unemployment system or the short-term disability system. In other words, they're naïve, so they work. They work hard. They work all day. They want money because they have to send it home. That was the deal about their coming in the first place."

In contrast, the ones that have been here for several years "work the system" whenever they can and take advantage of every opportunity to not work but receive some form of benefit instead." Further, he added, "They don't even report to work because they want money paid to them under the table, cash."

As a therapist, how do I keep my patient, the farm worker employer, to be honest and ethical in the face of so much disregard for ethics, honesty, and positive work experience by his workers and as encouraged by the government? Honesty and mental health are one in a kind. They go together. In therapy, keep honesty a central issue and good will follow.

MY COMMENT: Be honest and ethical even if those around you are not; that is the essence of integrity.

83.
SELF-EMPLOYMENT IS THE OPTION FOR SOME

In today's session with John, he indicated that the Court has just confirmed his charge of a felony related to a sexual offense with children. That means, his opportunities for employment have been significantly restricted, if not impossible. In some ways, Court actions create additional problems on top of the legal problem an individual is experiencing, and for which therapy is needed.

Talking with John today, regarding the charge and the actions in which he was involved, led me to the conclusion that his primary option for future work is self-employment. Working for an employer to whom he would have to disclose the sexual offense, appeared increasingly difficult and even unlikely.

For John, self-employment was interesting and unique, but very difficult. He comes from a history of "horse trading." Buying and selling off of the internet has been a long-term hobby of several family members. So, we talked about ways in which this type of work could be enhanced and maximized to the point that he could generate an income enough to live on. While there are many pitfalls in this kind of pursuit, it does represent an opportunity that could be developed immediately and not have to disclose his charge of a sexual offense to anybody.

Therapy is a place of creativity. Every patient presents a creative problem that demands a creative answer. I hope this creative answer will serve well for John as he moves forward and tries to make life a satisfying experience as well as a way to generate adequate support through self-employment opportunities.

Come what may, John still has to deal with the charges filed against him, but at least he can live in the meantime. It could well be a year before his situation is resolved with the courts. He simply could not live without some level of income. While it is true, he created his own dilemma, he cannot act in a manner that would make matters worse for himself and his family.

MY COMMENT: Even when circumstances are piling up against you, there are still avenues to pursue to keep life going forward.

84.
A SUCCESSFUL VENTURE REQUIRES A PLAN TO SUCCEED

Success is within reach of any person as well as achievement. However, to consistently succeed and achieve one has to remove and control the distractions to which they are exposed. and will take away their focus of attention and concentration.

This was the case for Joel with whom I met on six occasions. He was a young entrepreneur soon to graduate from university. He had a dream or vision of creating his own company utilizing his skills in computer technology. Joel spoke of his dream and it seemed reasonable. Joel spoke of the details, such as the financing and support that he would need to help the new company be a successful venture. Further, Joel spoke of the skills he needed to possess and yet develop, so he could be successful. In other words, Joel had a pretty good concept of what he wanted to achieve, but also what he would have to do, and the skills he would have to acquire so that his dream would become a reality.

The one thing that was missing in my conversation with Joel, which I pointed out in the third session, was his failure to account for distractions that were in his life at the time. So long as they were operating in his life, he could very well sabotage his very dream.

While we were able to identify several distractions, he was unable to identify some real and potentially dangerous distractions hovering around him and enticing him away from his dream. First, we commented about the girlfriends he has had over the previous five years, none of which were business-oriented or would have sacrificed anything for his success. Certainly, they never would have been a partner or companion in a business. This issue was a major source of potential failure.

Second, we spoke of his money management skills and attitudes. It became obvious that he was a spendthrift and that it was difficult for him to save money, for the sake of his future career rather than his current interests and needs. In other words, he was not able to sacrifice financially at this time for something important to him in the future.

Third, he had the distraction of video games and gaming. He was spending at least five to six hours a day gaming. That would never get him to fulfill a goal, no matter what it was. Gaming is an intense addiction that distracts from future opportunities, goals, desires, and dreams. So long as he is going to spend hours gaming, he would never achieve his goal for the business he was wanting to develop.

We took these three distractions, as well as others, and then talked about ways in which he could eliminate these distractions or manage them so that they were not self-destructive and self-defeating. It was a great lesson for him. By the end of the sixth session, he had a much clearer perspective on not only the goals that he was trying to accomplish, but what he would have to do to control the distractions so that his goals could be accomplished and realized.

The challenge was great, but his future was his call. Self-defeating behavior is a "death call" for any good we would like to achieve.

MY COMMENT: First identify your distractions. Then eliminate them or manage them to play a constructive role in your pursuit of happiness.

PART IX

CAN THERAPY HELP ME CLARIFY MY FAITH AND RELIGIOUS VIEWS?

85.
FAITH, TRUTH, AND LIFESTYLE CAN DETERMINE THE QUALITY AND LENGTH OF LIFE

How well and how healthy you live depends upon the decisions you make and lifestyle you desire. For example, longevity of life and the quality of life are related to the degree to which you keep your body moving, exercise, reduce and manage stress, eliminate or control alcohol consumption and all drug usage, as well as the degree to which you maintain an active and diverse social life.

In addition, there are other factors that contribute to life quality and longevity such as a lifetime pattern of a balanced diet and healthy eating. Further, it depends on maintaining a regular and personal involvement in faith development practices. This generally includes church attendance, Bible reading, prayer, a quiet time of meditation, and having friendships and faith-related discussions with those of a similar faith background.

As I meet with people in therapy, I find myself going through this checklist and adding two or three things that a person can do to improve the quality and the longevity of their life. Such conversation is often appreciated, as it was with Joe who was committed to change his ways and live a faith-based life. I always looked forward to Joe's next appointment, as they were always fun and stimulating.

Lists like this do not include things such as frequent visits to the office of your physician, how many degrees you achieve after high school, the number of friends in your circle of friendships, and how many dollars you earn above average income. While these things are valuable and often considered to be important, they are not essential for quality of life. One can live in poverty and have a high quality of life. One can live with chronic illness and still have a quality of life. One can live with few friends but still have a quality of life. Quality of life needs to include a practice of faith-based living.

EXPERIENCING PSYCHOTHERAPY THROUGH A ONE-WAY WINDOW

> **MY COMMENT:** Quality of life comes about through faith-based living.

86.
BEREAVEMENT IS PROCESSED BEST
WITH THE SUPPORT OF FRIENDS

Today, I saw a gentleman from India who came for an evaluation relative to immigration. He has legally immigrated from India to the USA and is now applying for citizenship.

During my interview, as I have experienced with many other individuals, the man spoke of the death of six family members in a very brief period of time and how devastating and impairing these deaths were to him. There are cultures, such as India, where death is a very personal experience and has very definite cultural implications for the spouse, parents, and the remaining family members. These are generally well-honored traditions and are deeply appreciated. Moving forward in his life was the focus of my sessions with him.

During my interview, as I have on other occasions, I was caused to reflect upon those in my life who have been very close to me and have died and left me with memories, many of which are very fond memories.

In fact, as I write this section of the book, I count 46 men who have died and absented my life and with whom I have had a meaningful relationship with over the years. Most of those deaths occurred over a very short period of time. Most people don't count the deaths that they experience. However, for me, it adds a level of appreciation and good memories of the people who have been a part of my life. The cumulative effect of these individuals, and their impact on me is once again appreciated by such recall of friendship over the years.

A piece of poetry has always been special to me as I process the death of a friend or family member. It goes like this, "God gave us flowers in the summer so we will have good memories in the winter." This poem causes me to reflect on the "flowers" of my life – friends, associates, family members, neighbors, church members, patients, and club members, to name a few. Some are still with me and in my life, others are no longer in my life in any meaningful manner. We are emotionally rich as we have many friends who share their life experiences and knowledge.

MY COMMENT: Enjoy your flowers when you can, even the memories of them.

87.
ANGELS COME INTO OUR LIFE FOR A PURPOSE

It is not uncommon for patients to reflect on events in their life and attribute those events to some type of power beyond themselves. Today, a young male patient attributed a particular profound event in his life that led him to believe that two angels had visited him.

I engaged in a discussion with him regarding angels, how he viewed them, how he defined them, how he would know when an angel appeared or not, and how would he know if it was the actions of an angel causing an impact on his life.

That led to my definition of an angel and I discussed it with him. It made sense to him and it gave credence to his story. I said, "An angel is someone that shows up, speaks up, and then scoots."

I have found that definition helpful over the years. It is not only understandable and helpful to patients, but has been found to be biblically consistent as well. It does take the mystique out of the concept of an angel for patients. It gives credence, gives understanding, and makes sense.

Now, I am not sure if any patient actually believes in angels after such a session, but many do indicate that my definition and our discussion was helpful and gave meaning to their experience. I have found that it also helps relieve anxiety and uncertainty for many patients.

MY COMMENT: Welcome angels into your life, but know the difference between an angel and other sources of influence.

88.
FAITH IS LIVED BEST WHEN SHARED WITH OTHERS

It is not uncommon during the course of a week of therapy to have numerous occasions to encourage patients to persist and endure the hardships and struggles of their life with which they suffer. Giving a word of encouragement to a patient such as, "Keep the faith," is a powerful statement in and of itself, but it often comes across as being simplistic and shallow. However, the statement in its essence is profound. It means something different for every patient. When I use it, I always take time to discuss it as to what it can mean in the life of that patient.

"Keep the faith" suggests that one maintains one's religious faith, nourishes it, builds it, and lets it become a full life support system. Besides just keeping the faith, it is important to understand that this statement also implies that one strengthens the faith of an individual and encourage even greater strength and persistence for the days ahead.

"Keep the faith" also suggests endurance, persistence, commitment, and perseverance. There are times when we all feel like giving up, but keeping the faith means, stay with it, stay the course, see it to the end, and maintain hope going forward.

MY COMMENT: "Keep the faith, utmost."

89.
RELIGIOUS FAITH DIFFERS FROM SPIRITUALITY

It has long been the general understanding that the personal faith of a therapist is to be kept either out of the therapy room or kept to him or herself and not be raised as part of a therapy session. While that may be true and be appropriate in many situations, there are, however, many patients who come with a very troubled religious faith history and background that complicated their life and contributed to the impairments of their life and their relationships.

In such situations, it is appropriate then to include one's personal faith and church participation history as topics on the therapy agenda. A therapist needs to be prepared to raise such issues when and as appropriate.

However, when the topic of faith comes up and is relevant, it is important to keep the focus on the patient's faith, not the therapist's faith experience. The therapist needs to be knowledgeable and conversant on the topic of faith and religious matters of all faiths, especially of those frequently presented in therapy.

This is precisely why a therapist needs to be also educated in sociology, comparative religions, and anthropology. Unfortunately, few therapists are so educated. If such issues are important for a patient, and the patient's issues cannot be objectively faced, the patient needs to be referred to someone who can address these issues.

It is my general practice when it seems that a religious faith issue is relevant, that I raise the question for discussion. I might ask, "What is your own personal experience with the church or religion?" Or, I might ask it in a different format, "Where is God in your life?"

I found both questions to be non-offensive to patients. In fact, most patients find this a very intriguing topic for discussion and enter into discussion quite openly and freely. It is my desire and goal in therapy to clarify and to clear-up areas of disparagement, hurt, and trauma in all areas of life, including the areas of church experiences and religious belief.

Most patients find it helpful when I draw the line of distinction between religion and spirituality. Spirituality has to do with the level of faith of an individual and how it is incorporated into his life. It is how he lives a life of faith that enhances his relationship with God.

On the other hand, religion is a relationship with the church or the formal structures of the church. Spirituality is one's relationship with God himself. A person may have one but not the other. Some have both.

From such discussion with a patient, I try to resolve past hurts, clarify misunderstandings, and help bring about a realistic and meaningful spiritual understanding for future church involvement and one's faith journey.

MY COMMENT: Know where you stand in your own faith journey and work to advance it, while helping others come to terms with their faith journey.

90.
WE LIVE ON FAITH AND MEMORIES WHEN DEATH PREVAILS

Today was unusual in that two separate individuals came for their regularly scheduled session during which they reflected on the recent death of their spouse. Both used the time to grieve. Both used the time to reflect and to resolve to move forward and to live a life of honor in memory of their spouses of many years.

During their two separate sessions, I reminded them of a piece of poetry that has meant a lot to me. I have had several occasions to share with others this poetry at a time of grief. It's important to reflect on helpful thoughts and advice from others when we need it. Here's what I shared.

"God gives us flowers in the summer so we have good memories in the winter." During the separate sessions, we spent considerable time identifying the flowers of their life, the flowers of their marriage, and particularly the flowers of the deceased spouse. Flowers come in the form of friendships, special memories, unique gifts, accomplishments, children, grandchildren, and very important times of solitude and intimacy.

Unfortunately, we all have times of winter in our life. There are the times of trial, pain, discouragement, hurt, and disappointment. It is in those winter times and experiences in our life that we need to draw on our positive past and renew our strength. To be sure, we gain strength from the flowers we have had all summer in our life. What are your flowers? Who are your flowers? Remember, they are there for you to reflect on.

MY COMMENT: Take time and recall the flowers of your summer to make your winters warmer and more consoling.

91.
SUICIDE DOES HORRIBLE THINGS TO A FAMILY

Today Julie called for an emergency appointment. When I saw her in the later part of the day, she unfolded a story of a very good friend and a distant family member, both of which committed suicide. The deaths were unexplainable. They were unbelievable. Such death is unacceptable. As Julie unfolded the story, you could just see the desire to deny reality which is part of the grief process. The anger which is also a part of the grief process was fully displayed as Julie told the story of these two individuals in her life.

Her stories caused me to reflect. I had a family member of a patient commit suicide in 1975. I've not had another suicide among my patients until 2021, when this particular family member of Julie's committed suicide. Additionally, there were three other individuals in 2021, whom I knew committed this atrocious act of death by suicide. It is important to note that suicides generally increased considerably in 2020 – 2022.

While it is reality, part of life, and part of the experience of every therapist, it's still tough to digest, accept, and understand. One wonders what the actual situation was that prompted these persons to commit suicide. Suicide is always connected to something. It never happens in isolation or in some theoretical manner. Time always tells their story.

For Julie, my role was to help her talk about her feelings and process the loss of these particular gentlemen. She needed to explore what they meant to her and her family, and how she can now live without them beyond this experience. Most importantly, however, was to help Julie turn these events into "good grief."

Good grief promotes growth, development, and positive outcome, even from a most unfortunate situation such as suicide. We spent several sessions thereafter exploring ways Julie could advance her life and live beyond these dreadful events.

ALLAN G. HEDBERG, Ph.D.

To be sure, how Julie processes her grief can be an example to others facing this same type of dreadful experience. Perhaps she can then be an "instrument of peace" in the lives of many.

MY COMMENT: Every death has its sting; death by suicide has its own particular sting.

92.
WHERE IS GOD IN MY LIFE?

Today, I was discussing with a young man the degree of contribution different sources made on his life and contributed to the problems he was experiencing. After some discussion regarding the contribution made by his parents, his teachers, his peer group, and himself, our discussion then turned to resources available to him for healing, for restoration, for rehabilitation, and for the rebuilding of his life. We then looked to the resources available through his parents, extended family, employer, friends, and others.

After a period of discussion on these issues, I then paused and said to him, "And where is God in all of this? Do you blame God at all? Do you look to God for help and assistance in rebuilding your life? Is God a player in your life?" Was God involved in your current problems? Can He be involved? Will you let God have a place in your life and world view?

Those questions prompted an entire barrage of discussion related to his childhood experiences with religion and attending church as a child. There were many good, positive and helpful elements, and there were some elements that were troublesome.

At this point in our discussions, we had to end our discussion. We picked it up again a week later when I again summarized our earlier discussion and then posed the question, "Where is God in all of this?" We went for another entire hour of discussion.

It's often said that religion is not something people want to talk about and should not be brought up in counseling. Contrary, after over 50 years of experience in counseling thousands of patients, it is a welcomed topic. It is a topic of considerable importance in the life and experiences of people and it needs to be explored and discussed in a safe and reassuring atmosphere and relationship. In fact, this is probably one of the key issues in therapy for most people.

It is important to tie together past experiences with current events, future aspirations, and goals. Religion, church, and God play a huge role in this process and need to be discussed openly and freely.

Obviously, it is important that the therapist not impose any particular religious experience or point of view, but to help the patient come to terms with his own experiences, and where God fits into his life currently and for the future. It is important not to proselytize or try to convince somebody of any particular theological or religious position. It's the religious experiences and religious relationships that a client has had that need to be explored and made part of the healing, rebuilding, and rehabilitative process.

Helping a person find a deeper sense of spirituality out of their past religious experiences is a reasonable pursuit in therapy. In so doing, religion and spirituality needs to be separated and clearly understood.

MY COMMENT: Remember this, your God experience is different from your religious experience.

93.
A VISIT FROM AN ANGEL CAN BE LIFE CHANGING

It is surprising to me the number of patients that account for a particular event in their life by referring to angels. Most of the time they follow-up by saying, "I don't understand it and I don't believe it, but it must have been an angel of some kind." I found that the more "Catholic" an individual is, the more likely an angel will be referred to as a way to account for a particular event that is otherwise baffling.

It has caused me to study and read on angels so that I am able to share with them a perspective of angels and give credence to their interpretation while, at the same time, not necessarily affirming that their experience was due to an angel. That is yet to be known or understood.

Patients do appreciate an informed discussion about their unique experiences, such as an event caused by angels. In therapy, it is not my job to affirm why certain events occur, but to help a patient think it through and gain some level of peace as they attempt to understand an uncommon event in their life.

Essentially, angels show up, speak up, and then scoot. When I explain that to a patient, it makes sense. It gives them a sense of comfort and helps them understand they are not crazy for having an experience that is often understood to be outside the realm of reality.

Every therapist must understand that some patients really do believe in angels, so such a definition is to be taken seriously. This topic could be a turning point for a patient, so time is needed to let the issue sink in.

It is not the role of the therapist is prove a point or convince a patient of a particular point of view, but to help the patient come to peace about a disturbing event in their life.

MY COMMENT: Remember, angels show up, speak up, and scoot. Listen to them. Pay attention. Take their message seriously.

94.
HOW TO TELL A GOD EVENT

Periodically during a therapy session, a patient tells a story of a particular unusual life event that had a profound impact upon them. As they tell the story and complete the point they are making, I often raise the question, "Was this God? Was this a God thing?"

Today was no exception. A young man told of a particular event that changed his life during his late adolescence. He too raised the question, "Why did this happen to me? Was this God?"

I replied, To know if this is a God thing, consider the following conditions: 1) The event happened sometime following a very definite prayer that was uttered to God regarding this particular event or situation in your life; 2) The event happened due to some very unusual set of circumstances that cannot be explained in any other way; 3) The outcome of the event had a positive influence or effect on your life; 4) The timing of the event cannot be accounted for in any other way, and 5) God meant it for good, so look for and notice the good in the situation or event.

If any of these five factors, or any of the five in combination, were present at the time in that situation, it is likely that the event was a "God thing," so take it seriously. Learn from it and carry out whatever the message is for you. Live accordingly.

MY COMMENT: When unusual events happen, examine if they are from God.

95.
A LIFESTYLE BASED ON FAITH IS A WELL LIVED LIFE

How well you live depends upon the lifestyle you create and the decisions you make. For example, longevity of life and the quality of life is related to the degree to which you keep your body moving, exercise, reduce and manage stress, eliminate or control alcohol consumption and all drug usage, and the degree to which you maintain an active and positive social life.

In addition, there are other factors that contribute to life quality and longevity, such as a lifetime of a balanced diet and healthy eating. Further, it depends on you maintaining a regular and personal involvement in faith development practices. This generally includes church attendance, Bible reading, prayer, meditation, and having meaningful friendships with those of a similar faith background.

In therapy, I find myself going through this or similar checklists while adding two or three points of my own that a person can do to improve the quality and the longevity to their life. Such conversation is often appreciated as it was with Joe who, in therapy, committed to change his ways and live a healthier life.

Lists like this do not include things such as frequent visits to the office of your physician, how many degrees you achieve after high school, the number of friends in your circle of friendships, and how many dollars you earn above average income. While living a quality of life, one can also live in poverty. One can live with chronic illness and still have a quality of life. One can live with few friends but still have a quality of life.

Therapy is a place to be reminded of these facts and to help you bring about a lifestyle consistent with these factors and life behavioral patterns. A life well-lived with quality balance is a life worth living.

MY COMMENT: Healthy living is good living. Good living is honorable living. Honorable living is a life worth living.

96.
GOOD GRIEF, NOT JUST GRIEF

Without a doubt, we are living in a time of grief. In this past two years during the pandemic, I've had more patients come into therapy who were experiencing some phase or aspect of grief due to the death of a loved one. Death is a tragedy any time. However, during this pandemic, we have seen the tragedy of the death of young fathers, young spouses, beloved parents, and the death of close friends unexpectedly.

Grief is a natural process following the death of a loved one. It reflects the loss that one experiences at the time of death, loss of opportunity to build new memories, loss of close friendships, loss of companionship, and the loss of mentors in our life.

As a therapist, it is important to understand and know the stages of grief and to help an individual finally understand that grief unfolds systematically in five stages. It is also help for them to understand where they are in the process of grief at this point in time of their life, and then move them along to the next level of the grief experience.

Familiar questions relate to, "Why me?", "Why now?", "Why this way?".

While none of us is a stranger to grief, to be sure, it smacks as a sting when it does occur. Sometimes this is referred to as "the sting of death."

While therapy cannot remove "the sting of death," it can help process its sting effect and help a person overcome and also rise to a much higher level of living.

Saying "good-bye" is an essential and important step in the therapeutic process. Moving on is another important step. Being at peace is certainly the critical and important component of the grief process for everyone.

MY COMMENT: While death has its sting, grief can have its victory and new life.

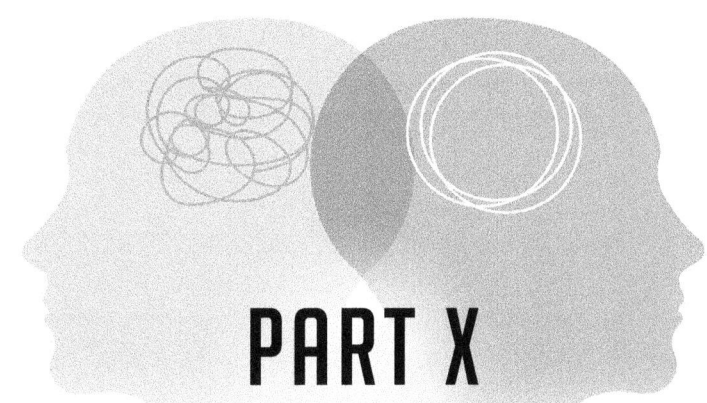

PART X

CAN THERAPY HELP ME LEARN IMPORTANT LIFE SKILLS TO LIVE LIFE FULLY?

97.
WHAT'S THE VALUE OF YOUR NAME?

Today, I saw a young collegian from the local university. He came into the office with a degree of confidence. What I first noticed about him from his clinical chart was his first name. It was his first name that I had never heard before. It was a very unusual name. It caught my attention and curiosity. I surprised him when I inquired about his name.

I asked him the meaning of the name and where its origins. He did not know the meaning, and he did not know where it came from. Usually, names that are uncommon and unique come from some source. The name of a grandparent, a cherished aunt or uncle, a biblical character, a historical character, or someone that the family admired at the time of the child's birth. We are usually named after someone or something.

After that initial interchange, we proceeded with the session as to the reason he came and how I could be of help to him. We had a good session together and ended on a favorable note. He seemed to be helped by our interchange over the course of the hour.

As he left, I admonished him to think of his name as being a good name, but that his name could never be worth more than he was. The person makes the name and gives it meaning. The person makes the name great. The person establishes the worth and meaning of a name, I told him.

The patient appreciated the comments and the advice and the thought that he was not only the owner of his name but the maker of its meaning.

After two weeks, he came back and indicated that he shared my thought about his name with his family and with a couple of close friends. It prompted a great deal of discussion among his family, none of which knew the meaning of his name or its origins. However, they all agreed that the name was going to be great and he was going to be worthy of it. He was personally encouraged by his family's confidence in him.

MY COMMENT: We make our name great by how we live and how we relate to others.

98.
THE SKILL OF DECISION-MAKING

In the course of therapy with a person, I often focus my attention on various structured areas for discussion that can be formulated in the making of a decision. There are always options. In one case, the decision is to go ahead and do it, while in another case the decision is to withdraw and do something else. However, one could always choose to live with the situation.

One of the things about people who are emotionally distraught and highly distressed is that they do not make good decisions. They often do not even have the knowledge and experience about the process of making decisions. Decision-making is a very unique aspect of life. It's an important aspect of life. It's a necessary aspect of life, and it brings life into focus. Decisions help sort out what we do and what we do not do, what we accept and what we do not accept, and what we allow or do not allow. Thus, it helps bring and keep life in focus.

Today, my session with a gentleman I have been seeing for a considerable number of months has been waffling on the issue of enrolling in law school. Should he go or not go? Should he do something similar or different? Should he be a paralegal, etc.? We have discussed all elements of it, trying to help him bring into focus that which is worthy of his time, effort and attention, and that which is not. I have tried to help him narrow down the aspects of a decision that would be favorable for his situation in the long-term as well as something within his range of capability and interest.

In one session, he indicated that he had made his decision and that he will, in fact, proceed to go to law school. Now, to me, it didn't matter if he went to law school or not, but what was important is that he made a decision, the decision was his, and the decision is something that is consistent with his heartbeat and his passion. We know that when a person has a passion and lives according to that passion and follows it, that they are much more likely to succeed, gain benefit, and enjoy the fruits of that decision.

In decision-making, it is important to identify the various options. Then it is important to weigh the advantages and disadvantages of the various options and the implications of those options. What a decision will mean for that person in the short-run, as well as in the long-run, must also be considered. It is important to look at the financial elements related to each option, as well. Then comes the delicate point of narrowing down the options from four or five to two or three, then to two, and then eventually to one. The decision to be made is ultimately the decision of the patient. My role is to guide, lead, encourage, and to raise provocative issues and questions to help bring the best decision into focus.

MY COMMENT: Life is better when decisions are made in consultation with a mature and wise person of value to you.

99.
GRATITUDE IS A HEALING AGENT

A young lady came today for her third appointment. I started out by asking what she would like to see accomplished in the next 12 – 24 months of her life. She had three answers, one of which was to reduce her depression.

After a time of defining her depression and understanding it better, I proposed the following. She should take down her home calendar from the wall and every day in the little squares on the calendar write down one thing for which she is grateful, I asked her to do that for 365 days and see how she feels after doing so for 6 – 9 months. Research indicates that this should and most likely will have a positive effect upon her mood, stabilizes her at a reduced level of depression that she now experiences. It could even remove her depression altogether if she were to stick with the "gratefulness plan."

In so doing, we defined gratitude as anything that happens during the course of the day for which she is thankful. This could be something very simple or very complex. Some days we are grateful for common things that we have been grateful for on many occasions and, at other times, we are grateful for some new experience or new idea that came to us. In other words, one thing we are grateful for can appear four or five times in the course of a month. The important thing is not what it is, but that we are aware of it and understand why we are grateful for something as we acknowledge it. I reminded her that research shows that people who maintain a gratitude journal tend to be less depressed a year later if they extend this practice for a lengthy period of time.

To reflect on gratitude experiences sets your mind in the right direction. It changes your mind from discouraging and depressing thoughts to thoughts that are more uplifting, positive, and happiness oriented.

Once we begin to have happy thoughts and regularly reflect on gratitude events, our mood changes and we begin to live more freely and kindly towards others as well as ourself. The process of happy thoughts and gratitude is profound and needs to be taught to every kid in school and in the home.

MY COMMENT: Be a person of gratitude and share it with others. Both of you will be better for it.

100.
CRITICISM IS A SELF-DEFEATING ACTIVITY

Joel was severely and constantly criticized by his father for most of his childhood. He seemed to do no right. This went on for years. Try as he may, he could never attain the appreciation or affirmation of his father. His mother tried to make up for it, but she could never make up for a father's critical nature no matter how hard she tried. Fathers have a unique influence on a son, good as well as bad. It can be for the good or for the destruction of a son's life. The formula of criticism always comes out to be a lose-lose situation.

In my therapy with Joel, I emphasized seven main points in dealing with criticism. The points proved to be beneficial and helpful. Joel became a little bit more self-confident and resistive to the impact of the criticisms of his father on him from then on. Even though these points are applied after the fact, they can still be helpful to Joel as he deals with criticism going forward.

The seven points I emphasized were as follows:

1. In every criticism, there is something to be learned. As has been said before, "Thar's gold in them thar' hills."

2. Don't get caught up in a fight by making the battle bigger than it need be.

3. Don't react in such a way that your critic (father) will now become your enemy.

4.   Let the critic go without considering him among your deadly foes.

5.   The truth will always outlast any lie that has been told.

6.   Whatever the truth is, believe it. Live it, and let it be.

7.   Remember the adage, "Sticks and stones will break my bones, but names will never hurt me."

MY COMMENT: Use criticism only when it can be presented in a constructive manner.

101.
FORGIVENESS IS A HEALING BALM

Frequently in therapy, the issue of forgiveness comes forward as an important issue to be discussed, understood, and handled. It is not uncommon at all for people who come into therapy to have a history of anger and resentment about things that have happened in their life, and things for which they have never received forgiveness or even sought forgiveness.

For healing to take place, forgiveness must be expressed, received, and mutually dispelled. That is possible only if the person with whom there is anger and angst is still alive and in the patient's life. For others, it's not possible to achieve forgiveness with a person with whom there is angst and who has now moved, is deceased, or is no longer involved in their life.

Hence, in therapy there are two issues that need to be considered relative to forgiveness. First, how do you forgive somebody who is not available and is no longer in your life? Secondly, how do you forgive somebody who is in your life and is not receptive to forgiveness?

Should forgiveness ever be offered and reconciliation sought, there are several steps to undertake for understanding to occur? There is no fast-track to achieve forgiveness, however.

What are the seven steps of asking for forgiveness?

- ACCEPT THE FACT THAT SOMEONE HAS BEEN OFFENDED.

- ACCEPT THE FACT THAT YOU HAVE BEEN THE SOURCE OF HURT.

- ACCEPT THE FACT THAT YOU NEED TO APOLOGIZE FOR WHAT YOU SAID OR DID.

- ACCEPT THE FACT THAT SOMEONE'S HURT CAN BE HEALED BY YOUR APOLOGY.

- COMMIT TO NOT DOING IT AGAIN.

- COMMIT TO HELPING THE HURT PARTY HEAL AND RESTORE THE RELATIONSHIP.

- COMMIT TO LEARN SOMETHING FROM THE FORGIVENESS PROCESS.

While it is easy and tempting to skip a few steps in the forgiveness process, it only cheapens the process and little benefit will occur for either party.

Unfortunately, we see these "cheap forms of forgiveness" in the public arena when public celebrities say, "If I have offended anyone, I am sorry." This is not forgiveness at all. It is only an attempt to achieve "cheap grace" and look good.

MY COMMENT: We can forgive, even if we never forget the offense.

102.
BE TRUE TO YOURSELF IN ALL YOU DO

Today, I was talking with Michael who stated that his grandmother was having her 89th birthday, and he was being encouraged by his mother to send his grandmother a birthday card or gift. The problem, however, was that Michael did not like his grandmother. She was mean to him over his growing years, and he had no particular feelings of goodness towards her. What should he do?

First of all, be true to yourself, I said. If you want to be a person known for social grace and doing the right thing, then send a greeting to her. However, you also have to be realistic. If you don't feel particularly good towards her, it would not be honest to send her a lavish gift or gushy card. The point that I was making was to do what is comfortable, do what is right for the situation, and do what you will feel good about doing. You have to feel you did the right thing when it is all over.

After much discussion, we decided that the most appropriate way to send a birthday greeting to grandma was to text grandma a 4-word message related to happy birthday. We also agreed that he should not say things that he does not believe or does not feel, but just be true and be gracious.

I then went on to talk about how he needs to establish a pattern for himself for years ahead. No matter if he gets a card in return or a thank you note in return, do what is right for you and how you want to be known. Generally speaking, it would probably be good to regularly send a card to people who are in your family and you are close to them as well as close friends. A message of congratulations, when appropriate for example, is always a reasonable thing to do. If you do it, keep it very conservative. Keep it brief. Be honest and sincere.

I ended our discussion by the issue of making sure that he does not try to overstate a message to grandma or anyone else, but to just send it and feel he did the right thing. Send a brief message. Don't try to elaborate or create some kind of an image where you're trying to sell yourself, make yourself look good, or say something that is not true. The important thing is, deliver the message of congratulations, but don't try to oversell the message or yourself. Honesty always pays off in the long run.

> **MY COMMENT:** Be true, be honest, be sincere, and be forgiving.

103.
SUPPORT PEOPLE ARE NEEDED AT TIMES OF LOSS AND HURT

It is not uncommon for a patient to come to therapy at a time of great trauma and other critical times such as the loss of a loved one. This was the case of Jill. As a result of the pandemic, she lost a very dear grandfather and a sister with whom she had a very close and loving relationship.

In such situations, therapy cannot begin until there have been adequate and abundant expressions of empathy, caring, compassion, and deep personal regret for the losses. Many therapists are unable to express the needed empathy at such times as they themselves have never gone through such an experience or lack of empathy themselves. Other therapists are by nature somewhat cold and unfeeling. At such times, they have a loss of words and the absence of feelings, to be sure.

Just what does one say? Every patient wants to hear a particular expression, a particular phrase, a particular emotion from their therapist. To be sure, words of expression, especially at great times of trauma and loss, are to be expressed very uniquely, personally, and sincerely. Only then can therapy begin and progress.

Just what are some of the words that a therapist might express in such a situation? How about, "I deeply feel for you at this time of great loss. I can't imagine what you must be feeling at this time in your life." Or how about, "Your loss is monumental. It's a unique experience that you're going through. I hope I can be of support, and I also hope that others have been able to be of support to you."

Of course, there are things not to say, such as "I feel your loss" or, "I know what you're going through. You'll get through it." "You're strong and you'll make it." These are trite statements and give little support. They are more offensive than anything.

Platitudes and assumptions are certainly unwelcomed at times of trauma and great loss. A therapist cannot be cold, unfeeling, and full of platitudes and well wishes. This is certainly a time calling for sincere remorse and empathy. This is what a soul-mate is all about.

MY COMMENT: Learn to express empathy in a sincere and caring manner; it is expected of a therapist at times of loss and hurt.

104.
A LIFE WELL-PLANNED CAN BE LIVED FULLY

I met with Cicero recently for five sessions as he was planning to soon go to a college somewhat distant from his home. His parents were nervous over his new opportunity for independence. He was excited, but had mixed emotions. He was the first of his family to leave home and go away to college, so it was a big event.

Over these five sessions, I talked considerably with him regarding the idea of planning. Planning his academics. Planning his social life. Planning his set of boundaries. We also spoke of his commitment to a life of honor and his family values.

He agreed that he was going to honor his parents and their support of his schooling. Planning how he was going to stay connected with family and many other areas of independent living was the focus of each session we had together. I tried to instill within him that success and achievement results from planning. A satisfactory life results from planning. A life well-lived results from planning. A life protected from impulsive decision-making comes from planning also.

Over the five sessions, he got the point of planning. Now it's up to him to live it out and reap the benefits that will come to him as a result of planning his course of life over the next decade, not just for his four years of college.

At our last session together, he spoke of the advice of his grandfather. It was profound. Grandpa said, "Don't' do anything that will change the course of your life forever." We had much fun discussing the meaning of that statement. Profound it was!

MY COMMENT: A life well-lived is a life well-planned.

105.
A FOCUSED LIFE RESULTS IN GOOD OUTCOMES

As a therapist, I am committed to living a life consistent with positive mental health, effective social relationships, and a kindly personal manner. This is true whether I'm in the office with a patient, relating to my colleagues or family, or relating to the general public as I come and go throughout the community.

Today was no exception. I was in the gym preparing to do my exercises and had an interchange with the staff member checking me in. I knew that he is a student but not in school or his program at the present time. I knew he planned to return to school next semester. Periodically, I encouraged him to keep in mind the importance of his higher education and its benefit for the long run for him.

Today, I again approached the topic of his preparedness to return to school this semester. He said he was. I commended him for that and then I added a discussion point of saying "this is where you are supposed to be." Schooling is important and he's supposed to do it for his own sake as well as for the sake of his family. He seemed to resonate to my repeated phrase, "Be where you're supposed to be."

That is true for all of us. It is important that we pursue a path of understanding of where we're supposed to be at any given time. The benefits will follow.

As you know, it is easy to be somewhere else than where you need to be or are supposed to be at the time. To get out of the pattern of life and not be where we're supposed to be is easy. It's so true for many of us. I repeat, "Be where you're supposed to be." Focus. Focus. Focus. Then, good things in life will follow. The misdeeds and trouble will diminish and go away.

MY COMMENT: Be where you are supposed to be. Focus. Focus. Focus.

106.
DON'T RUN DOWN PEOPLE AND DON'T RUN UP STAIRS

In my session with Andrew today, we focused on his chronic pattern and habit of criticizing others, particularly those in authority over him. In so doing, we traced his childhood pattern of being severely and chronically criticized by his father whom he is now replicating in his own relationships, especially in his workplace.

After much discussion on his pattern of behavior, I took particular caution to determine if he was being critical of his son as his father was of him. To some degree, this was true, but not to the severe degree that he experienced. We devoted one whole session to the ways he can prevent future abuse and begin to raise his kids in a positive and loving manner, despite his own experience as a child.

This then led to two or three sessions of anger management and especially anger expressed through critical comments. As part of my discussions with Andrew, I frequently used the phrase that I learned from my father, "Don't run up the stairs and don't run down people." This made good sense to Andrew as it was advice from a father to a son. We spent considerable time dissecting the meaning of this particular quote and how Andrew could apply it in his life.

After the third session, I didn't see Andrew for about three months due to circumstances. But when he returned to therapy, it did give us opportunity to discuss if he had applied that particular piece of advice over the three months. Happily, I learned that he did so reasonably well. Not totally, but he was learning to apply it and did so on numerous occasions. This gave opportunity for me to encourage him to continue and to make that particular quote his own. He could use it to guide his behavior with younger men and use it to guide his behavior with all people with whom he has contact.

He did not need to live a life of criticism and he did not need to replicate the way his father treated him. In his relationships with his friends, his associates, and his family, he gradually learned to avoid critical comments and be a person of shared joy.

This issue is so true for so many people. We tend to imitate our own parents even if they are incorrect, abusive, addicted, or dysfunctional in their life. We have to learn to stop such generational behavioral patterns and learn to live productively and correctly no matter how our parents raised us.

MY COMMENT: Treat all people with respect. To help, picture a clear visual image of a staircase in your mind.

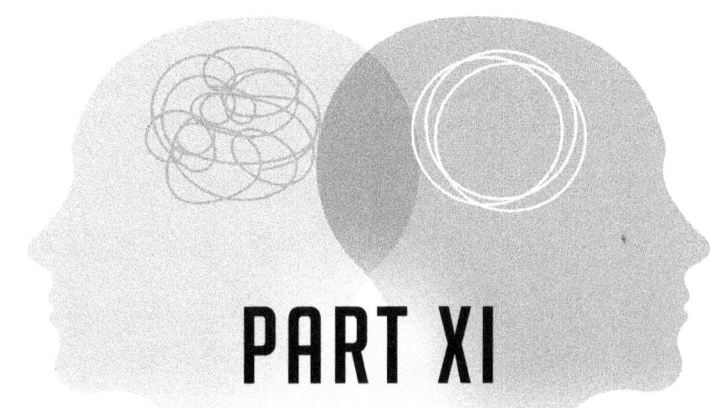

PART XI

CAN THERAPY HELP ME KNOW HOW TO HELP MY KIDS DO WELL IN SCHOOL?

107.
A QUALITY EDUCATION DEPENDS ON THE SUPPORT AND INVOLVEMENT OF THE PARENTS

Today, I was talking with a father from an Eastern country regarding his two children who are excelling in school. We talked about the factors that may be contributing to their strong and positive grades and commitment to education. The father said this, "I tell my kids that they're as smart as anybody else and others are as smart as they are." He went on to say, "That's not the issue. The issue is one of attitude. They go to school with an attitude to learn and to make it a good day." My wife and I both believe that and encourage it with the kids.

I joined in and then talked about the issue regarding attitude as well as the issue of focus. One has to learn to focus attention, focus energy, focus purpose, and focus the outcome of education. Once you focus, you then have the ability to use all your resources and all your ability, strength, and wisdom and apply it for good.

First, get the kids to believe in the good of education, the good of family life, the good of the general community, and for the good of the country. That's attitude, pure and simple.

Secondly, help the kids see how a good education and good grades will pay off now as well as in the future. What are the benefits of a good education?

Thirdly, model a good life before the kids. Help them see how education helped you and can now help them.

Fourthly, praise and reward all levels of success and accomplishment in the kids. Success is worthy of much praise and approval. Affirm all levels of accomplishment.

A life lived like this as a parent before your kids and instructing them accordingly will pay off and be repeated by the next generation, to be sure. It also depends on consistency by the parent and from child to child.

MY COMMENT: Praise and success encourages even more success.

108.
LEAVING HOME FOR COLLEGE IS A TIME OF ANXIETY FOR THE PARENTS AND THE STUDENT

Today, I was talking to Robert whom I have been seeing for five sessions in preparation for his leaving home and going away to college. Many topics related to independent living and personal responsibility were discussed at considerable length. Today's session was no exception.

In our session today, I asked Robert if his parents have given him any particular advice as he plans to go away to college. His answer was very interesting and intriguing to me. He stated that his stepfather said, "You're young, go have fun, do things that are unusual and different, but don't do anything that would be life-changing." As we discussed this issue, we enumerated several examples of what could be a life-changing experience that he would definitely be wise to avoid such as getting into some type of legal trouble, driving under the influence (DUI), creating a pregnancy, and experimenting with various forms of drugs. Any and all of these behaviors can be easily contributory to a life that becomes marked with addiction, depression, dependency, loss of freedom, and the loss of future opportunities.

I commended his stepfather and mother for giving him this particular piece of advice. There is a realm of behavior that can be engaged in, but there is always a limit and there's boundaries that need to be honored and respected.

This is a good life lesson as well not just for a young kid going off to college. We all would be better if we learned to live our life within the context of the boundaries that are reasonable, appropriate, and wise to honor and obey. It's best to set our own boundaries but certainly we can, by our passivity, leave it to others to set boundaries for us. Like it or not.

Dad was not only right, but he was also wise.

MY COMMENT: Go and have fun and live life fully, but don't do anything that will be life-changing.

109.
SCHOOLS TODAY ARE OFTEN OUT OF TOUCH WITH THE VALUES OF THE HOME

In the middle of a session today, a young mother of a fourth and fifth grader became agitated and distressed as she was caused to tell me about Critical Race Theory (CRT) being propagated in her children's school against her knowledge, wishes, and permission. She unfolded a story of the distress that her children were experiencing in the school. It became evident in their discussions about school that the children were often distressed when they reviewed their day in school. This was repeated over several weeks and on several occasions.

The mother gave the example of her children being placed on one side of the classroom while other children were being placed on the other side of the classroom equally divided. One side was told that they were to assume that they were white and that they were the oppressors. The other side was told that they were to take the position of being the oppressed black people.

The mother indicated this is never how she was raised and it was not how she is raising her children. To divide the world by color or by how people are treated is absolutely contrary to her values. She always taught her children to treat people equally and positively and to make friends of all children. As she spoke, she grew increasingly angry about what had happened to her kids in school.

The school was outrightly creating a conflict in her home as it was also doing in so many homes of the kids in that classroom. The mother went on to say that CRT is not true. She noted that this was not the way America was formed and it was not how people were treated over the years. It certainly was not her experience growing up as a child in school or in her community.

The mother went on to state that contrary to her child's teacher, America is not an evil society needing to be fundamentally transformed. Contrary to the teacher, she has always taught her children that there are no oppressors and oppressed, but all are equal, all have equal opportunity, and all need to be encouraged equally. She went on to say that she has always taught her children that America is not a racist society or system and she did not want them to be that way either.

The mother was now faced with a dilemma, to leave the kids in that school, take them out, or go to the school and raise a ruckus and try to get this type of anti-American teaching stopped. By the end of our session, she had not yet decided what to do, but she did have options and she was exercised enough to take one of her options and work it out.

Her time in therapy with me was most fruitful. We need to see more of that from our mothers and our fathers and not let the schools go off on a tangent of untruths and then blindly teach them to our children. Teaching subjects and the manner of teaching needs to be consistent with the values of the parents.

At that point it became clear to my patient that the teacher no longer was a teacher but now was a propagandist, the voice for Marxism in modern day American education. This was eye-opening and disturbing, to be sure.

Are teachers that dumb and do not see through the unproven and unsupported propaganda of this Marxist movement in America, the mother asked? Unfortunately, teachers have now lost value in the eyes of this mother and others, to be sure.

MY COMMENT: Parents need to stand together and speak up together as one voice in the community and not just about school related issues.

110.
HIGH SCHOOL GRADUATES MUST ALSO GRADUATE FROM HIGH SCHOOL BEHAVIOR

Each time I meet with a high school graduate, as I did with Henry, I look for opportunity to discuss a very important concept that each high school graduate must consider. I always ask when they graduated from high school. The date is well ingrained, and they answer without hesitation.

I then follow up that question with a follow-up question which is not so easily answered but provokes a lot of discussion. The follow-up question is, "When did you graduate from high school behavior?" Often, they're not even able to answer the question but it does provoke good discussion. I encourage young people to seriously look at that issue and begin the process of breaking away from the high school patterns of behavior and enter into the world of independent adulthood.

This discussion often involves the enabler issue. Parents enable high school and immature behavior. Parents need to learn how to withdraw from that kind of inappropriate support and enablement. The question begs the discussion of newer and more mature friendships and the overall selection of better and more mature standards of living, post high school..

MY COMMENT: When you graduate from high school, do so academically, socially, behaviorally, and emotionally.

111.
LEARNING A FOREIGN LANGUAGE IS A USEFUL SKILL

It is not uncommon, especially in California, for patients to be referred for therapy who speak a foreign language. Generally speaking, I as a therapist am unable to provide the service as I do even if I do or do not speak a foreign language. However, there are times when an interpreter is utilized. If it involves legal issues, then a professional interpreter is generally considered and hired.

If it is a personal issue and just a matter of a native language, then informal arrangements can be made with family members or a relative who speaks a foreign language and experiences a strain in all relationships in the community because of the difference in language being spoken. However, that is not really what I want to talk about. What I would like to say is this. When a patient comes for therapy, even with the use of an interpreter, they do appreciate being complimented for their use of the English language even though it is broken English. They appreciate being encouraged to continue the course of learning the language and acquiring it informally as well as through formal educational opportunities.

I always try to teach the patient one or two English words or expressions as a way to have fun and encourage the learning of English. The patients like engaging in this little exercise.

Here's a piece of advice that foreign speaking patients appreciate hearing. It is based on an old Chinese adage and it goes like this – "If you speak a foreign language, a smile overcomes the majority of the strain, stress, and disconnect that is experienced between two individuals from different cultures and ethnic backgrounds."

It is important that I take considerable time to smile and how to encourage the patient to smile also. When to smile? How long to smile? And, how to smile genuinely.

Now that's a lesson for all of us. We don't have to be a foreign language speaker to appreciate the role of a smile. We can all benefit and we all can provide the benefit of a smile for others.

Learn to smile and do it often, but do it sincerely and genuinely. A smile puts other people at ease. It opens the door of relationships. It brings people together. It connects people. It puts you at ease. It puts you in the role of an influencer upon others.

MY COMMENT: Smile but make it real and sincere.

PART XII

CAN THERAPY HELP ME OVERCOME MY ADDICTION?

112.
ADDICTION IS HARD TO ADMIT

Am I addicted? Today's session was with a young man who was referred to me for counseling by his attorney as he had just received his third DUI (Driving Under the Influence). In my discussion with him regarding his drinking pattern, I became quite aware of the fact that he was not accepting the idea that alcohol had become his area of addiction and it was becoming more engrained in his behavioral repertoire. We outlined the pattern of his drinking from high school onward. To be sure, he was addicted as per the addiction pattern of drinking.

Finally, in the session, I felt it was important to define addiction as I felt that he was misunderstanding the nature of addiction. I proceeded to identify the primary components of addiction. We talked about each of the addiction characteristics as it relates to him. I noted two major points of addiction: Alcohol addiction is easy to achieve and it soon becomes an obsession.

In today's session with Jennifer, the issue of controlled drinking was raised as a topic of importance as she was already experiencing in her early 20's a life of alcohol addiction. Self- control was becoming harder to achieve. She already had one DUI and was living a life that would very certainly bring her another DUI and perhaps another after that. She did not know how to control her drinking.

To assist her in making a decision regarding her future drinking, we spoke of the options of abstinence and control drinking. She did not like the idea of abstinence.

In regard to control drinking, I indicated that there are three guidelines that are generally helpful to individuals committed to a controlled drinking program. They are:

1. Drink no more than two drinks in any given drinking episode. It is the third drink that changes your attitude, mood, and personality pattern. Avoid number three altogether.

2. Drink by the numbers. A bottle of beer is a bottle of beer. A glass of wine equals two of beer. A shot of liquor is equivalent to three bottles of beer. Again, use the policy of never drinking beyond two bottles of beer in a drinking episode. That equals one glass of wine.

3. Drink only beer that contains a low volume of alcohol. Choose the light of the lights.

Addiction is clearly evident by the drinking behavior or the drinker. The signs include the following:

1. There is a historical pattern of increasing the amount of alcohol consumed over time before you get to a point of satisfaction or the state of inebriated.

2. You become emotionally distraught and upset, agitated when alcohol is not available or you are prevented from drinking.

3. You become agitated when alcohol is withheld or you are prevented from drinking.

4. In the absence of alcohol consumption, you become consumed with the notion of seeking out alcohol, getting access to it, and consuming it. A definite "search and seizure" behavior pattern takes place.

5. Alcohol is a primary topic of discussion and pursuit among you and your friends.

6. In the absence of alcohol, you become obsessed with getting more of it.

7. Withdrawal effects are profound.

8. Your primary life patterns and choices revolve around and include alcohol consumption.

MY COMMENT: Drinking is addictive: you are not your own for evermore.

113.
TURN YOUR BACK ON MARIJUANA AND WALK AWAY

Today was marijuana day for some reason. My 10:00 appointment was with a 50-year-old gentleman who had a 25-year history of drug addiction, including alcohol, marijuana, and a variety of other drugs. As a result of his addiction and resistance to any treatment, he lost a professional baseball career, occupational opportunities, a marriage, and a portion of his brain.

In other words, through our discussion it became very evident that he was experiencing the damage to his brain typical of individuals with a long history of alcohol and marijuana usage. Memory loss, attentional loss, and thought processing loss were all indicated. He believed he had a bipolar disorder. It became clear that he did not have a bipolar disorder, but one of addiction with associated brain damage and the associated grief due to the losses in his life related to his addiction.

At the end of the day, I met with a young 23-year-old who since age 14 had used marijuana every single day, numerous times throughout the day. He confessed that he was high when he came to the appointment. He was high every time I met with him. He states he has never been without the influence of marijuana in his system since age 14.

The pattern of a 14-year-old was exactly the pattern of the older gentleman that I saw earlier who was now 50 years of age reflecting the detrimental effects of chronic use of marijuana.

It's like most addictions. The person must be ready to walk away from the addiction-based lifestyle. If there was anything I could do or try to break his addiction thinking and help him come to the position in his life where he would be ready to live without it, I would have done so. As in all addictions, it is a "state of readiness" in the patient to change that is critical and needed. That is the role of the therapist in working with individuals such as these two men in how to help them come to a point in their life where they believe they can live successfully without the dependence on a substance.

Addiction is real and powerful. Man is weak and vulnerable. This is no behavioral pattern to take lightly. The long-term dangers, risks, and losses are significant.

MY COMMENT: There is a time for everything, even a time to walk away from an addiction or potential addiction.

114.
WE ONLY GET A FEW OPPORTUNITIES TO START OVER IN LIFE

There are very few times in a person's life when they can make a major change or adjustment in their lifestyle and patterns of living. Yet, many of us live our life hoping and waiting for an opportunity to do what you have always wanted or do something different and special. Unfortunately, it usually does not happen because of the lack of time, money, or the personal resources to pursue a lifetime dream.

There are only a few times when one has the opportunity to start over or set a new path. These times are few and far between. For example, graduation is often a time for a new directional experience. A major change in life may also come at stressful times such as divorce, losing one's employment, retirement, or a disability from a trauma or accident to name just a few. In other words, there are several natural events which give opportunity to capitalize on and go in a new and different direction.

There are obviously great benefits that comes to those who take the opportunities life presents and reorganize their life for future fulfillment. For example, we make new friends, new learning experiences, the realization of a life dream, improved health, and re-invigorating one's own marriage and family life are also a few possible benefits of moderate and reasonable risk taking at critical times in life.

If you are in a situation where you have opportunity to fulfill a dream or set a new course for your life, I would urge you to get serious about it, plan it, and go all out and make it happen.

Now let me say this, the stable and successful management of one's addiction is another great time to start over and begin a new life. Let me underscore the basic principle, the successful management of one's addiction is first required. One does not go in a new direction to conquer an addiction. In such a case, the addiction goes along with the person only to repeat itself in a new location. Indeed, a new direction comes after the addiction has been conquered.

A few safeguards need to be considered. For example, there needs to be adequate funding of the venture. The venture should not place you or anyone in your life at risk. Success needs to be a reasonable possibility. Also, there needs to be a positive and well-established support system in place to assure ongoing sobriety.

MY COMMENT: A support system may be needed throughout one's life to assure ongoing success. Embrace it!

115.

SOME NEW ADDICTIONS ARE EMERGING

Over the past several months, I have had occasion to interview six or seven individuals who are adorned with numerous tattoos and/or bodily piercing. As I speak with these patients in therapy regarding their decision to engage in tattoos and body piercings. I have learned of several underlying themes that promote such behavior and sustain it over time. Upon my review of the answers generated from these interviews, a distinct profile similarly seen in the various addictions also prevails among those who make tattoos and body piercings a major part of their life.

Here are some of the features that are enumerated by those with tattoos and body piercings suggestive of an addictive process taking place in the same way that one experiences addiction to alcohol, drugs, gambling, shoplifting, overeating, sexuality, and other self-defeating addictions:

- The financial funding of tattoos and piercing is taken from a person's general budget that would ordinarily contribute to a quality of life for oneself as well as one's family. In other words, it is diverted money much needed elsewhere in one's budget. The cost is generally in the range of $300.00 – 700.00 per bodily impression.

- Obtaining a tattoo or piercing is usually followed by emotional elation, but short-lived and can be re-generated when thought is given to the next tattoo or body piercing. In other words, it's use is generally associated with emotional arousal.

- A period of elation after obtaining a tattoo or piercing is generally followed by a time of depression or flattened affect. It is this state of depression that promotes the desire for another tattoo or piercing.

- There is a planning stage for the next tattoo or piercing of days or weeks as a person plans his next tattoo or piercing. An emotional experience or high is experiences as to purchase the next tattoo or piercing.

• There is usually the desire for more bodily stimulation, one after another. Life is built on the planning of the next tattoo or body piercing. There is no end. One is not enough. Two is not enough, and then three is not enough. On it goes.

• Tattoos and body piercings jeopardize one's employability and social relationships. Many employers will not hire persons with such adornments. Body adornments also distances a person from other people, thus jeopardizing the number and level of depth of relationships in a person's life.

• The withdrawal syndrome is also present. When one cannot or is not able to obtain another tattoo or body piercing, for whatever reason, a general withdrawal experience is a person's reality. Such moods of depression are then altered, changed, or overcome by planning, anticipating, and obtaining another tattoo or body piercing. The cycle of addiction goes on and on and on.

• As in all addictions, many engage in the behavior to a small extent, with only 10-15% become fully addicted. All are at risk, however.

• There is a planning stage for tattoos and body piercing of at least days, weeks, and months as a person plans his next tattoo or body piercing. An emotional arousal or high is experienced as the day approaches when the next tattoo or body piercing can be arranged and purchased.

• There is usually an ongoing desire for more, another one. Life becomes built on and organized around the planning of the next tattoo or body piercing. There is no end. One is not enough. Two is not enough, and then three is not enough, etc.

• Tattoos and body piercings can jeopardize one's employability and social relationships. Many employers will not hire persons with such adornment.

• Adornments also distances a person from other people, thus jeopardizing the number and depth of relationships in a person's life.

- The withdrawal syndrome is also present. When one cannot or is not able to plan for and obtain another tattoo or body piercing, a general withdrawal experience is a person's reality. Such moods of depression are then corrected, altered, or overcome by planning, anticipating, and obtaining another tattoo or body piercing. The cycle is common to all addictions. No cycle can be completed without the ability to have or find the financial resources to pay for the next tattoo or piercing. The cycle is compulsive and demanding.

- As in all addictions, many engage in the behavior to a small or large extent, but only 10-15% become fully addicted. All are at risk, however.

It should be noted that there are certain personalities and patterns of life that are more prone to an addiction of tattoos and body piercings as we see in alcohol and drug addiction. As in most addictions, it involves people who are socially introverted, socially isolated, socially depressed and socially anxious. Whatever is done to overcome such emotional states through tattoos and body piercing does not resolve and will not resolve such emotional states whatsoever. It is a false hope.

It should be noted that tattoo and body piercing in themselves create these very same kinds of problems or intensify one's social-emotional distress. Such behavior further isolates and separates an individual from his peer group and the general social society.

Unfortunately, such behavior tends to motivate one to seek out people similarly situated to the point that they become a subgroup of people unto themselves. The adage applies, "Birds of a feather flock together." Hence, the very behavior patterns engaged in to improve one's social status and social acceptance only contributes to further downgrading of one's social status, social acceptance, and social support.

Unfortunately, therapy with those already "tattooed up" is usually an exercise in futility. On the other hand, those who are not given to tattoos and piercings can be a force for good towards those not yet caught up in the wave of addictive behavior.

Further, for individuals considering such behavioral choices and options, I would hope that they would stop and consider the underlying motivations and emotional states that are involved in this kind of behavioral pattern.

Depression can be solved in a much better and healthier ways. Social anxiety, social withdrawal, and social isolation can be improved in many different ways that are much more healthy and less self-destructive.

It should also be seriously considered as to one's future life and life experiences yet to come. Tattoos are forever. However, one's emotional states, goals, ambitions, and opportunities vary over time. Hence, there will be time in the future when tattoos and body piercings interfere with and deny one of the opportunities that may lead to a much greater level of social, mental, occupational, and personal success and recognition. Tattoos and body piercings can and often do contribute to one being stuck at a lower level of aspiration, achievement, relationships, and growth opportunities. Reaching one's potential is at risk to be sure.

Lastly, tattoo and piercing removal are now becoming a developing business. Many with tattoos and piercings want to give up their false dreams of valor, their immature ways, their gang identification, their anti-social ways, and their false hope for a new and better identity. They want to start over and take a better path and build a life of admiration and opportunity. Simply stated, they are ready to move on and integrate into society, find meaningful employment, and reconnect with their family and community in a meaningful manner. More power to them.

As one young man put it, "It feels like the right thing to do, like I'm forgetting the past and moving forward to a brighter future." Another, young girl said it this way, "I'm thankful for this program because it's helping me erase a mistake that I never thought I could."

Think about it before tattooing or piercing.............

MY COMMENT: Behold, all things become new.

PART XIII

CLOSING THE WINDOW

CLOSING THE WINDOW ON THE THERAPY SESSIONS

One does not enter therapy to address a specific problem and leave the same person. Change occurs in therapy. Sometimes the impact is significant and dramatic, while at other times and for some people the impact is of limited value. There are several factors that come to play in the making of a positive and effective therapeutic intervention and experience. Psychological research tells us that the following four factors are very critical for effective therapy to take place:

1. A positive and compatible relationship between the therapist and the patient.

2. The patient comes with an expectation of gaining benefit and that significant change in their life will take place.

3. The more years of experience and skill of a therapist to address the presenting problem of the patient the better.

4. A patient must like and trust the doctor and the therapist.

In other words, every therapy is not the same. Every therapist is not the same. Every patient is not the same. Every presenting problem is not the same. Each of these components must be addressed as a unique component in the overall interplay that takes place during the therapeutic 50-minute hour.

When does therapy end? When does the window close? That is a decision made primarily by the patient, but is usually and commonly a mutual decision made by the therapist and the patient together. Is more therapy needed? Is more therapy desired? Is more therapy necessary?

Overall, a therapist has an ethical responsibility to provide the right therapy to the right patient in the right manner for the right amount of time to bring about the right level of change and improvement in the life of the patient. Therapy is not meant to go on and on. Generally speaking, both the therapist and the patient know the unique time when therapy has been effectively concluded and needs to now be terminated. Essentially, therapy is terminated, not the patient. An ongoing open relationship prevails between the therapist and the patient into the future as need might arise and as new situations occur in the life of the patient.

It should also be noted that there are times when only little benefit occurs. Sometimes no benefit. In such situations, we go back to the four components noted above. Any one of those absent that could result in an ineffective and non-beneficial therapeutic experience for a patient.

Of course, there are other extenuating factors as well such as the development of new problems that are bigger and more profound than the ones being addressed in therapy. Or, a bad therapeutic session takes place and inadvertently creates a conflict or tension between the therapist and the patient. In such situations, it may be wise to terminate therapy and refer the patient to another therapist that can address the issues more effectively and more specifically and personally.

A person should never be intimidated or made to fear changing therapists for any of a number of reasons. It is not only the right of the patient, but it is also a proper action, at times, on the part of the therapist.

MINI-LESSONS IN LIVING THE UPS AND DOWNS OF LIFE

MISFORTUNE HAPPENS TO ALL OF US: Rise above it and don't let it overwhelm you.

WHAT IT'S LIKE TO BE BETRAYED BY A FRIEND: Betrayal is one of our most painful events.

LONELINESS IS NO FUN: Yet, many live a life of lonely desperation.

WINNING IS ALWAYS BETTER, BUT LOSING CAN BE A GOOD EXPERIENCE ALSO: Hard to believe.

BEING IGNORED, ESPECIALLY BY FRIENDS, IS PAINFUL: It is an experience like loneliness.

PAIN CAN HAVE A REDEEMING VALUE: But the lessons learned are hard fought.

SUCCESS REQUIRES THE SUPPRESSION AND DISREGARD FOR DISTRACTIONS: Focus is essential.

SUCCESS MEANS THAT YOU MUST FOCUS ON THE ESSENTIALS: Every situation is different.

ACHIEVEMENT REQUIRES THE ENDURANCE OF TRIALS: We all walk our own path, often alone.

SUCCESS REQUIRES THE ATTENTION TO THE GOALS AND PRIORITIES: We set our own goals.

SUCCESS MEANS THE DISCIPLINE TO FINISH WELL: It is necessary to start, but one must finish.

FOCUS ON THE ESSENTIALS: Eliminate the distractions so the essentials are in clear view.

DEVELOP A MIND-SET TO ENDURE TESTS AND TRIALS: The race is not based on speed.

INCREASE YOUR ATTENTION TO THE GOALS AND PRIORITIES: To those you have selected.

HAVE THE SELF- DISCIPLINE TO FINISH WELL: It is not based on speed, but endurance.

NOTE TO THE READER

In the service of confidentiality, I have heavily disguised each patient's identity and story by using an alias name, changing their story on a few identifiable points, adding a few fictional statements into their stories, and even combining stories of two or more patients who had similar stories and experiences.

Almost all patients are from my clinical practice but span a course of time, over 25 years as I have been able to remember the key issues and teaching points.

Each of the 116 vignettes tell a story and is included for its teaching lessons for all of us to learn to live better lives and raise better families. Each vignette is a mini-lesson for the reader. It is always a good thing to learn from others and even the mistakes of others. Indeed, I learn something every day and from every patient. It really is a cycle of experience….passing it on and learning from each other. Truly, that is, "giving psychology away," the theme of my professional career.

OTHER PATIENTS ARE NOT TO BE FORGOTTEN:

- Countless couples were seen over the years regarding the stability and future of their marriage. Two lessons stand out: Most couples know what to do to fix their marriage, but just don't do it, and most couples want a simple fix in one or two sessions. Never did I tell a couple to divorce. The research says, stick it out five years, you will be glad you did.

- What do parents do about their kids who are obsessed over gaming and/or social media. It is not uncommon for kids today to spend 6-10 hours a day on the various devices. Here is the rule, three hours a day is recommended and then the cell phone or x-box or computer is put away until the next day. Further, gaming is preferred over social media. Parents need a system by which the kid's technology is place on hold and the kids can rent it or use it by the hour after the three hours have been fully used.

- Online dating and marriage have become more common in the last few years. I am often asked of my opinion. Yes, but be careful. Double check and verify what is said or represented by the other person(s). Four marriages out of four via the computer systems have been verified to be good and reasonable. Computer based dating is still a high-risk activity. It is more common today, however, and most people are more experienced today than 10 years ago.

- Patterns of diagnoses change over time. Lately, we have seen more autism among adults as well as kids. We are better at diagnosing it today. It is now being included in the educational program for most psychologists, so they know it now when they see it. We also have better treatment options and know what to do and what not to do.

- The plague of drug addiction has become more common incrementally. Not only kids, but many parents and adults. It is common for someone on drugs at the time of their therapy session to talk during the therapy hour and I not know very much of what they were talking about. To be sure, drugs impair thought, relationships, conversation, emotional expression, to name a few distinct affects. Once therapy progresses, the interaction during a therapy session improves because drug use either stops or greatly curtails. Therapists have to be on guard for violence when a patient is using drugs and has done so for a long period of time. Drug use and violence go together, unfortunately.

- Husbands, boyfriends, fathers, brothers and most men are still reluctant to come for therapy themselves or in support of their wife, girlfriend, mother or significant other. This is one reason die before women. They avoid medical and psychological care and advice. However, when a man does come alone or with someone in his life, the benefits are usually positive and beneficial for all. This remains one of the major paradoxes in relationships.

- Life has many hard realities – trauma, untimely death, chronic pain, rejection and abandonment, parental failure, violence, abuse, and conflict, to name a few. It is common for such realities to prompt someone to seek out a therapist, and rightly so. It is usually the place therapy starts and then proceeds to other issues long overlooked. It is like the old adage says, "Don't let a crisis go to waste."

- We now know more about medication use for people experiencing depression, anxiety, anger, and other such emotional states. Consider the primary research finding that guides our treatment approach when medication is under consideration. Medication alone is the least effective course of action, psychotherapy alone is usually a good and much better way to go, but psychotherapy along with a brief use of a low dosage of medication is usually a reasonably good and beneficial course to undertake.

- Who do I seek out for a therapist? That is a tough one for everybody. Ask others who have gone to therapy for a recommendation. Call a few offices and ask a few questions that are important to you. Go for one session and then decide to continue or not. Seek out the opinions of others – pastors, teachers, nurses, doctors, friends, and read the website of several therapists. Not all therapists are the same or even good for you. Check out the websites of several therapists. Good and experienced therapists for usually well known in a community. Ask about the various options. Here is a guide line – older in age, experienced in practice, graduate from a well-respected university, specializes in patients your age and with your particular concern or problem, and has an approachable and friendly office personnel and manner when you call.

- All breakups are hard to process. But, the breakup of one's first love in high school is especially tough. This is when parents and teachers need to be particularly observant and involved. At such times, self-destructive behavior, such as cutting, and suicide attempts are much more likely to occur. Having a relationship with a therapist before such even is occur is best, but don't delay in obtaining professional help at such times as these.

- Conducting therapy is particularly challenging with physicians, nurses, dentists, counselors, teachers, and professional peers. It is difficult for such professionals to experience the turning about and now become the patient - the one seeking advice. A therapist must take charge and yet be sensitive to the difficulty of a "provider of care" now becoming the "receiver of care." If this barrier can be resolved, therapy can be highly successful despite professional differences.

- It is common for patients to report on their most recent dream. Dreams are of significant interest to most patients and most have a particular dream to report. Patients want you to take a stab and interpret the dream. I usually help patients understand the purpose of the dream and their importance. Briefly, dreaming at night is the brain's way to integrate some experience with all of one's prior experiences. The brain seeks to bring together all of our experiences into one whole theme or storyline. Trauma, especially is difficult to integrate and make sense out of it. Psychological peace requires the integration of all of life into a whole, a whole and meaningful theme or storyline.

PART XIV
APPENDIX

COMMENTS FROM COLLEAGUES

Once again, Dr Hedberg has written a practical, helpful book. Both the general public and persons interested in becoming a professional will find this book to be insightful and thought provoking. Dr. Deborah Ohanesian, Fresno, CA

In this book, Dr. Hedberg shares his experiences and insights from over 50 years of professional practice in clinical psychology. Therapists and patients alike will find much wisdom here. *C. Eugene Walker, Ph.D., University of Oklahoma*

Dr Hedberg "passes on" his therapeutic insight, depth of knowledge, and realistic problem solving by allowing the reader to see through the window and observe therapy in the real world. Mike Fitts, Psy.D., University of Arkansas for Medical Sciences, (Retired)

A novel idea and way to help other patients and graduate students learn the therapeutic approach to healing and wellness. David Senn, Ph.D. Clemson University

Dr. Hedberg's book provides insight and understanding to how the therapeutic process works to help those who are first time patients or those who have anxiety about entering therapy to address person issues. It is also an excellent tool to help those engaged in therapy to make the best use of their time and gain the most from it.

Also, this book should be a must read for any psychotherapist in training to help them understand how the therapy process works. For the therapist, it provides a structure with ideas for approaching treatment for most clinical situations. Michael Kesselman, Ph.D., Fresno, CA

WHERE AND WHEN DO I READ THIS BOOK?

- ON THE PATIO
- IN THE BATHROOM
- IN THE CAR
- ON THE BEACH
- WHILE WAITING FOR THE KIDS
- WHILE WAITING FOR THE TRAIN TO GO
- IN THE WAITING ROOM OF THE DOCTOR
- BEFORE GOING TO SLEEP
- AFTER YOU TURN OFF THE TV
- WHILE RFELAXING
- WHILE WALKING ON THE TREDMILL
- WHILE ON THE STATIONARY BIKE
- .....JUST TAKE IT WITH YOU WHERE EVER YOU GO

CONNECTING WITH DR. HEDBERG AND LEARNING MORE

BOOKS BY DR. HEDBERG

- LESSONS FROM MY FATHER
- DEEP ROOTS
- DOCTOR, TEACH ME TO PARENT
- OUT OF THE DARKNESS OF DEPRESSION
- LEGACY: A PLACE TO PARK MY STORY
- LIVING LIFE @ ITS BEST
- KIDS ALIVE
- JONATHAN EDWARDS: A LIFE WELL LIVED
- BETTER PARENTING
- ACHIEVING AND LIVING A HEALTHY LIFESTYLE IN A WORLD OF STRESS

(All books can be ordered through Amazon, Barnes and Noble, directly from my office,

or from my web site: www.booksbyhedberg.com)

LISTEN TO DR. HEDBERG TALK ON PARENTING, FAMILY LIFE, AND TOPICS ON PSYCHOLOGY AND DAILY LIVING

thepsychologyreport.buzzsprout.com

You Tube: Allan Hedberg

You Tube: Doctor, Teach Me to Parent

You Tube: Psychology For Today

You Tube: From Boys to Men

You Tube: CentralValleyTalk.com

MEDIA CONNECTIONS WITH DR. HEDBERG

E Mail: allanghedberg@gmail.com

Twitter - @Allan Hedberg

Web Site – www.booksbyhedberg.com

Facebook – Allanghedberg.com

FAX: 559 - 244 - 3261

PHONE: 559 - 244 - 3260

THE AUTHOR

Allan G. Hedberg is a clinical psychologist in Fresno, California and has served as a psychologist in a variety of capacities over 50 years. Besides serving as the treating psychologist for over 1000 patients, he has taught psychology students in six universities in the United States and Canada, has lectured on psychological topics in four different countries, has authored over 150 articles and 14 books, hosted radio and television programs and now hosts a popular pod cast, Psychology For Today, and is frequently consulted on legal issues and cases by attorneys and the Courts.

After 50 years of professional practice, he now bids adieu to an active practice, but remains active in writing, consulting, and lecturing. Psychology has been his love and passion as a profession and way of life. His life theme has always been, "to give psychology away." He derived great joy in knowing others benefitted from his input and experience.

Finally, Dr. Hedberg is overjoyed to know that many of his graduate students over the years have done well and have also been effective contributors to the quality of life of their patients, their respective communities, and to those in their spheres of influence.

- DO YOU KNOW HOW TO BE A FRIEND AND GAIN FRIENDSHIPS?

- DO YOU KNOW HOW TO OVERCOME DEPRESSION?

- DO YOU KNOW HOW TO IMPROVE YOUR SELF-ESTEEM?

READ THIS BOOK AND LEARN HOW TO IMPROVE YOUR SOCIAL SKILLS IN DAILY LIVING AND IN YOUR IMPORTANT INTERPERSONAL RELATIONSHIPS.

IF YOU ARE A NOVICE THERAPIST OR STUDENT STUDYIING TO BECOME A THERAPIST, THIS

BOOK WILL SERVE AS AN ADVANCED COURSE OR SEMINAR IN PSYCHOTHERAPY.

www.ingramcontent.com/pod-product-compliance
Lightning Source LLC
Chambersburg PA
CBHW051510120626
46551CB00012B/864